The Floyd Mayweather Mind

Learn the simple secrets that transformed struggle into success

From Reemus Boxing

D1523204

Publisher: Independent Publishing Network

Name: Rahiem Bailey

Company: Reemus Boxing

Email: Reemus@reemusboxing.com

Please direct all enquiries to the author

ISBN: 978-1-83853-615-2

London, United Kingdom

www.ReemusBoxing.com

INTRODUCTION

TABLE OF CONTENTS

INTRODUCTION

INTRODUCTION

"Well my goal in life, which I know is going to happen, is: I'm going to retire as the best fighter ever" - Floyd Mayweather, 2005

Ten years after Mayweather made this statement, he got the opportunity to prove himself right by competing in one of the most significant sporting events in history. On May 2nd of 2015, the two best fighters of their generation squared off - Floyd Mayweather against fellow Hall-of-Famer and long-time nemesis Manny Pacquiao.

This bout with Manny Pacquiao was initially expected to take place in 2009, but after many unsuccessful negotiations, boxing fans had to wait an agonizing six years before seeing 'The Fight of the Century' take place. It was set to be the most lucrative fight in boxing history. This event was so huge that the previous failure to negotiate the fight successfully was named 'Event of the Year' in 2010 by *The Ring* Magazine.

But, what made this event so huge was not just the fact that both fighters were regarded as the best of their generation, but that many considered Pacquiao to be the last remaining fighter who could defeat Mayweather. However, the fight didn't exactly follow that script. Just like Mayweather's previous 47 fights, Pacquiao could not solve the puzzle of Mayweather's incredible defense once they got inside the ring.

For the most part, Mayweather was untroubled by the threat of Pacquiao, and the fight failed to live up to the hype. It was a peculiar situation for Mayweather.

The match was widely considered to be a disappointment, primarily due to Mayweather's superior skills, which made it more one-sided than fans would have liked.

Afterward, he spoke about the lose-lose situation he was in, saying: *"If I would've fought Manny really stupid and reckless.. ..you know what the fans would've wrote today, and the media would've wrote today? [They'd say] 'Floyd fought dumb, I don't know why he didn't stick to his game-plan!' "*

It truly is a testament to Mayweather's level of greatness that the prospect of him losing had become such a sought-after event. Though many boxing fans tuned in to see a display of talent and action, many simply tuned in to see Mayweather 'finally' lose.

Many had come to view Mayweather's undefeated winning streak as somewhat intimidating. His achievements alienated him from the everyday-person, most of whom fail to reach anywhere near such heights. The idea that someone could hold so much power and win so consistently represented a threat to the inhabitants of mainstream society.

It gave them the motivation to see Mayweather lose, so they could feel like he was 'humbled' back down to their level. This is not uncommon. It is widely known that fans will support you on your rise, but wish for your downfall right when you reach the top.

However, what many people don't realize is the fact that Mayweather is not so different from the rest of us. He started no different from any of us. The beginnings of Mayweather's life were humbler than that of the average American.

It was hard work that harnessed the talent he had and allowed him to achieve 'The American Dream'. And in addition to a tough personal life, Mayweather's career was also a struggle.

The 300-million paydays that Mayweather received are what many people fixated on, as Mayweather's career came to a close. And, understandably, these thoughts may evoke feelings of envy. But what many of these people forget is that the early part of Mayweather's career was a struggle for stardom. It required a tremendous fight, both in and outside of the ring for Mayweather to even be in the position to receive such huge paydays.

Once you understand Floyd's early career struggles and see what it took for him to get to the top, you can begin to truly appreciate his achievements. After doing this, the feeling of being alienated from his greatness transforms into something else. You may even start to feel as if you relate to him, gain a deeper understanding and be inspired to use the lessons he learned in your own life.

From a young age, Mayweather felt that he was destined to become the best fighter ever. And as of 2020, after three years of retirement, fans contently accept that Mayweather was one of the greatest fighters ever.

Mayweather became known as a cocky fighter, who many believed had an inflated ego. He was criticized for being arrogant and overconfident. But Mayweather preferred to see it only as 'belief', and the result of the knowledge he held deep down of what he was capable of achieving.

The intriguing thing about Mayweather was that he seemed to know exactly how great he would become. Everything he did was to carve out the career that he felt he deserved to have. While he is loved by some and hated by others, one thing is for certain - he earned the respect of the majority.

To come from where he came from and face the obstacles he faced, yet still achieve what he achieved, is nothing short of a magnificent feat. However, he is often discredited by critics who disagree with some of the routes which Mayweather took. There will always be that one fight that 'Mayweather avoided', or an opponent he faced that could've been closer to his 'prime'.

Truthfully, no matter what Floyd did, there would've always been a lack of satisfaction from his critics. And the sad thing is, this subtracts from the credit he truly deserves and by discrediting his success in this way, we rob ourselves of the opportunity to learn from his triumphs.

This book aims to dissect some of the unspoken principles that contributed to Floyd Mayweather's success. We'll observe some of the critical moments of his evolution, and show you how you can apply it to your development.

There are four main areas which we look at:

- Developing an insane **work ethic**
- Harnessing your **skill level**
- **Marketing** yourself to the world
- **Cashing out** on your work

As you can see, these principles may also apply to those who do not box too. For example, Floyd Mayweather's media marketing abilities may help entertainers of other kinds. Or perhaps Mayweather's handling of business may help the average guy to improve on his financial situation.

At the beginning of each chapter, there will be a collection of quotes that are from Floyd Mayweather. It captures his thought patterns regarding the relevant topic in an authentic way. These are not quotes that I have simply copy and pasted from Google.

I have directly written down most of the quotes presented in this book, after spending countless hours diving deep into the lesser-known archives of footage on Floyd.

There will also be 'Champ-Tips' throughout the book. These are practical tips based on what Mayweather did to excel, and are presented in a way that you can directly practice in your life and career. Boxing is a beautiful sport, and the greatest gift it gives is the opportunity to grow. This book is a tool designed to aid that growth. It is designed to make the road to success clearer.

The greatness that was within Mayweather lives in all of us in some way. Having the right experiences was what allowed Mayweather to access it. I believe that it is a crime to live a life without having done what you can to access that inner greatness. So, as you read 'The Floyd Mayweather Mind' keep that in mind - you can be just as successful as he was in your own way.

Disclaimer 1: I would recommend that you read this book in conjunction with watching "The Rise of Floyd Mayweather". It is a documentary that details Mayweather's first 10+ years as a professional, and highlights the struggles he had to overcome to get the respect and stardom he deserved. It will help you get the most out of the book. It is available on the 'Reemus Boxing' YouTube channel.

Disclaimer 2: There are a few scenarios and stories which have been left out from this book, as the lessons may have been presented in my other books' The Cus D'Amato Mind' and 'Automatic Ambition'. This was done to avoid overlapping.

CHAPTER 1: MEDAL-WINNING MINDSET

QUOTES

Floyd Mayweather Senior: "Floyd knows everything about boxing. That's second nature to him. That's all we did our whole life."

On his father's influence on his upbringing:

"My dad was real harsh. I couldn't make no mistakes. If I made a mistake, my dad would cuss me out, slap me, check me, chastise me, put me in my place."

Floyd Sr.'s reply: "No pain no gain. See, that's something that I installed in him."

On getting into the fight game:

"All my life man, my whole life, everybody around me was boxing. I come from a fighting family. [At] family cook-outs, they know what it is. It's dancing and boxing."

"It's not just my talent. It's my family background. Both of my uncles were fighters, my dad was a fighter. That's all I ever knew, was boxing."

"Boxing is not something I wanted to do. Boxing was forced on me."

"If I had one bad day, he [Floyd Sr.] was always on my case. You know, always on my back. Stay on me. 'You're not doing good, it's not good enough'. What I never liked is that it was never good enough."

"[At] five years old I could run six or seven miles. And at that particular time when I was five, when you're at Kindergarten, you go to school for half a day. So, when I used to go to school, I used to get back at 12 in the afternoon. So, early in the morning my dad used to train, so I used to train with him."

"We built this body from the beginning to eat right, eat fruit, eat healthy, eat a healthy dinner everyday, drink water, exercise, and rest. We did this years ago. When I say years ago, we're talking about the early 80's. I was running miles and miles as a kid."

"Being smart, not taking no punishment, not abusing my body, getting rest, eating right. See, they think that everything just happened 19 years ago. No."

On his love for boxing:

"I don't know anything else but boxing. My whole life, I ate, slept, shit and drank boxing. That's all I did. I love the sport. I loved it so much."

"My main thing was I gotta get to the gym. No matter how late I stayed up or where I went, I got to the gym every day. But when I was that age, I thought nothing in the world was better than going to the boxing gym. Nothing. Every day. I mean, I wanted to go to the gym on Sundays. Going to the boxing gym was the best thing in the world. Because that's the first thing I know about!"

"I went to the 12th grade but I didn't finish school because I chose to put my mother in a better situation. Boxing was my girlfriend. Boxing was my life. Boxing was my wife. I said, you know what, school ain't worth it. I was tired, tired of my mother having second-hand furniture."

"My mother was spending her last money to give me a birthday party and my mother was working at a nursing home. So I said fuck it man, I'ma roll the dice and I'ma get on my grind and I'ma hustle. I'ma make enough money to put my mother in a better situation. And I don't want my mother to ever have to work again."

On his 1996 Olympic experience where he received a bronze medal:

"You lose gold, you receive silver and you receive bronze. I'm glad I got the bronze, because a true champion can take a loss and bounce back. And I feel that was my loss. That was God telling me I need to work harder. So when I got on the plane and left Atlanta, I left it right behind."

On his mindset towards training:

"I never quit and I never show fatigue. I'm always ready physically and mentally"

"I come always ready, no matter what fight [it is]. I don't care who I'm fighting. I could be fighting a guy who's ten [wins] and ten [losses], I'm still gon' be in the best shape. I'm still gon' train like he's the best fighter that I've ever faced."

"Certain fighters may be a lot better skilled fighters, more naturally talented, more skill, may hit harder. But the guy that puts all the work in in the gym, done all the running, done all the hard training, it'll show in the fight."

"In our gym there are rules: don't cry, don't complain, don't get tired, don't talk back to the coach."

On the way to a late-night training session:

"It's 1am, I'm going for my third workout. Do I want to go to the gym? Absolutely not. I'd rather lay in my house and sit in the movie theatre and watch movies. But to be the best you've got to work overtime. To be the best, you've got to work overtime."

On discipline:

"Anything can happen. That's why you gotta prepare all around the board. You got to prepare yourself all around the board. As the fight gets closer, I still work hard. I don't want to ever have that on my mind, that I didn't give my craft 100%. If you give anything less than 100%.... you're losing."

"At the end of the day, it's about who's more hungry. I'm going into the fight as the challenger.. ..I'm more hungry, I'm more dedicated. You will never catch me coming into a fight half assed. I'm going to come 100%. If I don't come 100%, I'm not coming at all."

"I train for every fight in the same way: I push myself. I believe in my skills and I believe in my talent. And I've been in there with the best. And the results are always the same."

"Any great basketball player that's out there right now, had a lot of great nights. But also had a lot of bad nights, but still is known as a great player. In this sport, it's different. You lose? You lose your number one spot and the L stays with you [for] the rest of your career."

"It's always about being at your best. It's always about pushing yourself to the limit, of course, being sharp and smart."

"I used to party every night, go to the strip club. But I used to always dedicate myself to my craft."

"I keep my eyes on the prize. I never focus on things outside the room. My focus is the guy that is in front of me. You get to where you're trying to get to by staying focused, staying on a parallel path. I always had a dream. And my dream was to always be the best...when it comes down to boxing, I'm the best at this."

"One thing about me, I've never overlooked anyone... ... I've never focused on things on the outside. I never put anything before I put boxing. This always came first. At 4:30 in the morning when my opponent is sleeping, I'm working. When he's up, working at 2 o'clock, 3 o'clock, I'm working."

"I don't want to leave nothing in this to say I wasn't the best. So no matter what the writers say, I don't read it anyway. It's not my focus. And I don't watch my fights, I don't have to. And if I do go back and watch it, I criticize myself and say 'you know what?, I could've got better in that department.'"

"A lot of fighters now, when they come to Mayweather Promotions, say 'we want a new car', 'we want a house', 'we want an apartment'. They want everything. But they don't really wanna put in the work. And I got to where I got to by putting in the work, sacrificing a lot of things. I left my mother in the hood until I was able to move her out the hood.. .. you have to sacrifice something to get something."

On his winning spirit:

"I strive to be a perfectionist every day. I work harder. No one is perfect. But one thing I can say is that I always find a way to win. I always find a way to win because I was born a winner and I'ma die a winner."

"No matter what it is, I always want to win. I'd pick winning over money. I could be playing against a NBA player in one-on-one basketball and I'm still going to think he can't beat me."

"The thing is this, with me in the sport of boxing, I was willing to die doing the thing that I love. So if you're willing to die to do something you love, 99% of the time you're going to come out on top. So, just like Kobe Bryant, Michael Jordan, you gotta take the shot, even if you miss."

"I will leave it in my skills. Even though the guy that I'm facing is good, I feel that I've put in the hard work and it's gonna show when we meet. And when we meet I believe that my skills will outshine his skills."

"Once I'm in here I go in the zone. And once I go in the zone, can't nobody stop me."

"It's not bragging, boasting, or cockiness, if you're going out there and producing. But if you talk, if you do a lot of talking but you're not producing, then that's considered bragging where we're from. So whatever I say I'm going to do, I'm going to do it."

"When we say 'push it to the limit', we truly believe there are no limits."

"I don't try to pick up a book [magazine] and see if I'm on the cover. Most of the time, it's fans who bring a book to me and I didn't even know. My whole life, the only thing I thought about was my craft."

"I dedicated myself to boxing. From morning until night, every day. I practiced day in and day out. Hours and hours and hours. Even like for a super fight, for a Pay-Per-View fight.. ..if I go to the boxing gym and I feel like even when I spar, if a guy gets the best of me in two rounds out of 10 rounds, I feel like I didn't do good. So I'm very, very hard on myself."

"I respect tennis and I respect golf. But this is not a gentleman's sport. This is boxing. We already know what this is. It's combat, we're at war. So if we're at war and you get a chance to get up on your enemy, you get to size him before y'all go at each other. That's what I'm gon' do. You know, it's like a routine. You already know what the results gon' be."

"When you go to war, you're gonna get hit. It's just how you react after you get hit. Do you fold, do you run for cover, do you quit, do you wave a white flag, or [do] you keep fighting? I keep fighting."

"I could care less what the weight is. I'm in there to fuck you up. I can care less because I know he's in there to do damage to me... .. he's in there to fuck me up so my thing is, I have to go out there and do damage. I was built for this. I like the smell of the gloves."

At a press conference, prior to facing Oscar De La Hoya:

"Like I said, Oscar's a hell of a fighter. He's accomplished a lot in this sport. But it's not about how many Pay-Per-Views you've sold, how many ex-champions you've been in there with, how many fans love you, how many fans hate you. When it's all said and done, this shirt's gotta come off me [he takes his shirt off]. That tight suit gotta come off you [as he points to Oscar beside him on the press table] and we gotta bang, toe-to-toe."

On having belief:

"If no one believes in Floyd Mayweather, Floyd Mayweather believes in Floyd Mayweather."

"From the beginning, from day one, I knew I was the best. I didn't have to second-guess. I didn't have to tell myself. I just knew it."

"All my life I knew that eventually one day I was going to be the best fighter in the world.

"Duran is a legendary fighter and I think Sugar Ray Leonard is a legendary fighter. There's nothing but respect. I take my hat off to those guys, but [do] you think I came in this sport and gave this sport 30 years of my life, just to put my mother out the ghetto and to move from a seven deep in a one bedroom home, and I worked so hard so my mother and my sisters didn't have to work, I gave this sport my life, just to say another fighter's better than me? Absolutely not. I'm not gonna say that."

"I respect them. But I'm not going to sit right here and say 'he's better than me' because I've accomplished a lot, like they've accomplished. But I accomplished it in a different era. Back then you could fight 100 times, 120 times. In my era to build a fight of this magnitude, takes 4-6 months, that's half a year. So I'm only able to fight two times a year."

"Some say I'm cocky, some say I'm arrogant. I say it's high confidence. I truly believe in myself."

"When you're coming into my domain it's a different world. When it's a fight of this magnitude, I've been here before, so I know. Don't make no mistakes and always bring your A-game. If you slip in any department, you shouldn't be in the ring with Floyd Mayweather."

Talking to his daughter Iyanna, schooling her on success (as seen on the boxing docu-series *All Access*):

"Jealousy; people jealous of you, comes with success. So anytime you're successful, people are going to be jealous of you. People are not always going to like you.. Some people don't like you when you're in school right? But that doesn't stop you from going right? And you still go there and be your best. Same thing like my job. I still go out there and be at my best. As long as you love me, can't nobody beat me.'

Speaking of his critics:

"How can you criticize something you have never done before. So that's just an opinion that you've got."

"The thing is you've never seen me lose a round. So I could win 9 rounds, he could win 3 rounds and they're gonna say 'do a rematch', or 'Mayweather didn't win'. But I'm used to it, it's gone like that my whole career."

"It's never good enough [to satisfy them]."

On his success:

"I've been through a lot in my life. And I beat all odds to get to where I'm at today. I came from nothing and built an empire."

"You just never know what you can get in life if you work hard and dedicate yourself. I dedicated myself to my job and my job is to be the best at what I do, and that's boxing."

"This is me. Didn't nobody get in there and put the gloves on for me. Didn't nobody get on that road and run miles and miles for me. Nobody took the broken ribs, nobody took the bloody nose. I did it all. I dedicated myself to my craft and busted my ass."

"A lot of times you hear people say 'Floyd Mayweather is always flashing his money, he's always flashing his cars. He's always flashing his jewelry.' I didn't rob anyone for it. All I did was go out there like an American citizen and dedicate myself to the sport of boxing."

"Of course, the American dream is to make a lot of money and take care of your family and take care of your loved ones. So I always want my family to have the finer things in life. I'm a man, no different to anyone else. I'm giving back to the people I'm supposed to give back to. I worked hard, I earned it. So I'm able to spend it like I want to spend it."

"Is it about the money? Absolutely. Is it about the fame? Absolutely. It's everything wrapped in one. I wanna be the best, not just best fighter, I wanna be the best athlete. When I leave: I will be known as TBE, and that's The Best Ever."

PRIMED FOR GREATNESS

Upbringing

To truly understand the roots of Floyd Mayweather Jr.'s success, you must go back to his childhood environment. It was that environment that laid the foundations for his greatness, and it had begun being cultivated before he was even born.

This is best summed up by the late, great trainer–commentator Emmanuel Steward, who once said, *"I don't think there's ever been a[nother] boxer, from the day that he entered this world, that was groomed to be a boxer like Floyd Mayweather."*

Floyd's entire family had been heavily involved in the sport of boxing, even before Floyd's arrival into the world. Floyd was born on February 24th, 1977, when, as he put it, *"a superstar was born."*

In this period, Floyd's father and uncles were busy trading leather with some of the best fighters to ever grace the ring. Floyd's father had been a top contender in the 1970s. Floyd Mayweather Senior campaigned as a welterweight and had once fought the legend Sugar Ray Leonard, though this was before Ray Leonard became a champion. Despite the fact that Floyd Sr. did lose that fight, his grit, speed, and ring intelligence gave Leonard a stern test as they battled to a 10-round decision!

But the Mayweather family's boxing heritage runs even deeper than that - with Floyd Sr.'s brothers, Roger Mayweather and Jeff Mayweather also being fighters. Jeff enjoyed a decent career, competing for 9 years, winning the minor portion of the world title belts and even earning the IBO super-featherweight title. He went on to fight the rising Mexican-American star Oscar De La Hoya (who later fought Floyd Mayweather Jr.), though he lost that fight in 1994 via a fourth-round TKO.

But it was Roger who achieved the most success out of the three. Roger Mayweather became a two-weight world champion and was known as the "Black Mamba." That nickname was earned thanks to his multiple victories over Latino fighters.

Roger won the WBA/lineal super-featherweight titles and the WBC light welterweight title in the 1980s. He'd been in the ring with the legendary likes of Julio Cesar Chavez (twice), Pernell Whitaker and Kostya Tszyu.

The world that Floyd Mayweather Jr. entered into was different from that of the average fighter, even considering those who had also come from generations of boxing. The outstanding male role models that guided him provided a wealth of experience. Even if just one of those ex-fighters were to coach a kid, then that kid would've been lucky!

The luck of Floyd Jr. was plentiful, as he benefited from the knowledge that all three could pass down to him. From the birth of Floyd Mayweather Jr., the best possible conditions were in place to help him become "The Best Ever." All he had to do was take advantage of it.

Though he eventually became the richest fighter who ever lived, he started from humble beginnings. Floyd has never been shy about this and has let the world know how deprived his early life was.

Floyd was born in Grand Rapids, Michigan. But he spent the 1980s in New Jersey, where he lived with his mother and siblings "seven deep in one bedroom and sometimes we didn't have electricity." But poverty wasn't the only deprivation he had to endure. Family feuds and an unstable home were also synonymous with his childhood.

Floyd Jr. was just a baby when his father was shot in the leg by his uncle (on his mother's side). Floyd Sr. had been holding his son when it happened. Floyd Sr. used baby Floyd as a shield, knowing that the baby's presence would deter the man from shooting him fatally in the torso. This shooting tragically ended Floyd Sr.'s boxing career.

On looking at Floyd's childhood, his success is even more striking. This is a reality he is very aware of, once stating that, "When people see what I have now, they have no idea of where I came from and how I didn't have anything growing up." The cards were dealt against him. Those who endure similar childhoods usually never end up accumulating even a shred of the success that he later gained.

Before Floyd Jr. had plans of growing into a fighter (and before he was even old enough to know what a "fighter" was), it was Floyd Sr. who held those aspirations for him. The moment that Floyd Jr. was strong enough to stand upright, his enthusiastic father put those little arms to fighting use. As a young toddler, Floyd Jr. was encouraged to play-punch doorknobs around the house, and the youngster mimicked his father's every move.

By the time little Floyd was 4 years old, his father already had him in the boxing gym, punching the speed bag. Floyd Sr. held the youngster up so that his little arms could connect with it. And if being in the gym wasn't enough, the

Mayweather family spent family gatherings play-boxing each other. Floyd was always around boxing, and this was the catalyst for the pugilistic education he was destined to graduate in.

A Young Prodigy

Floyd's first amateur fight came when he was 10 years old. The then-64-pounder ignited the start of his 84W-6L amateur record (there are also reports of his record being 84-7 & 84-8). It was clear from the very beginning that he was a young prodigy on the rise. Training at the *Tawsi and Pride Boxing Gyms* in Michigan, Detroit, Floyd won three national Golden Gloves tournaments (at 106, 114 & 125 pounds).

Dave Packer, President of the Michigan Golden Gloves, described the young Mayweather as *"being able to do what a 19-year-old could do as a very young boy."* He had abilities that no one in his age group had, and his defensive sagaciousness earned him the nickname "Pretty Boy."

Though many think that Floyd Jr.'s DNA was the driving force behind his success, this is not the case. As discussed, Floyd's training began from the time he could walk. From around 4 years old up until 16, Floyd Sr. trained his son before he went to prison. And the value of being taught by Floyd Sr. was in the fact that Sr. was both a great motivator, and a knowledgeable teacher.

Floyd Sr. knew what it would take to perform at the highest levels as he had experienced professional fighting himself. Floyd Jr. was the perfect opportunity for him to correct all of his mistakes. And he certainly made little room for error as he pushed Floyd Jr. to the absolute edge in training.

Floyd Sr. was extremely militant in disciplining the young fighter grew up. As Floyd Jr. put it: *"If I had one bad day, he was always on my case. You know, always on*

my back. [He would] stay on me. 'You're not doing good, it's not good enough.'
What I never liked is that it was never good enough."

The standards for Floyd were extraordinarily high and his father disciplined him harshly to maintain it. In response to that, all that Sr. had to say was, "Look at him today." And we could definitely all agree that such sacrifices paid off in the end.

Floyd's sisters later spoke of how their brother didn't get to hang out as much as the other kids. Floyd didn't get to experience a normal childhood like other kids because his father ushered him to the gym. If Floyd couldn't find the will to push himself on days that he was exhausted, his father would call him a quitter.

The father-son duo traveled across the country, visiting different boxing gyms so that Floyd could gain valuable experience with various styles of fighting. The training that young Floyd received was as brutal as it would've been for a seasoned pro champion.

Without a doubt, such standards increased the quality of Floyd Mayweather's training. And this is to be expected as everyone knows the value of "hard work." Though Floyd didn't like how harsh his dad was on him in the early years, it gave him a work ethic that made him the most disciplined fighter in boxing history. More than anyone else in the sport, Floyd grew an appreciation for the grind of success.

However, there was another type of "work" that his father gifted him. It is the type of work that is under appreciated when compared to "hard work," but is just as important. It is "smart work." Floyd Jr. worked hard because of his father's militant attitude. But in addition to his hard work, Floyd also worked intelligently.

Smart Work – Trickle-Down Expertise

It wasn't just the intensity of the training that was high quality. The tricks Floyd Jr. learned from his father were also of the highest quality. This combination of hard work and high-quality feedback from his father created an almost-perfect fighting machine.

Much of your boxing education starts with a good coach. A coach is your mentor, and their mission is to relay information to you in such a way that makes it easy to execute. Mentoring is also vital as it speeds up the learning progress. The role of a coach is an essential one, and he must have significant experience in the area you want to excel in.

As Floyd stated:

> "A lot of times, these coaches are inexperienced because they've never been in that situation. I don't want no trainer in my corner when I'm fighting if he ain't never been in a fight before. You gotta have some type of experience in fighting."

Many great trainers have not had a massive amount of success as a fighter themselves, and this is not a big deal. However, they must have at least a little personal experience as a fighter so that they have a better understanding of your point of view. Additionally, it is best if your coach has had a lot of exposure to other high-quality coaches (or fighters) who have attained success themselves.

When facing new challenges that require a specific approach, it is important to consider bringing in new expertise. This could mean bringing in a new addition to the team, as either a significant replacement or a minor secondary addition.

Coaches all specialize in different areas, and that is the beauty of variety. Do not cling to the idea that you should only benefit from the knowledge of one particular coach. Always remain open to new perspectives from other sources of experience and wisdom if the situation requires it.

This doesn't necessarily mean you have to replace your leading coach though. Floyd Mayweather never replaced his original trainers (Floyd Sr. and Uncle Roger), but he did switch between them when he felt it was necessary. He also brought in new expertise by enlisting 'spies' in some of his fights.

Mayweather has publicly claimed that he had inside intelligence and private information such as: how many rounds his opponent had boxed/sparred, what his opponent had done in training and how they were dealing with managing their weight. Though Floyd was always confident in his chances of winning, this information allowed him to tailor his game plan for an even better chance of winning.

In 2017, Mayweather fought the popular MMA-fighter Conor McGregor in a boxing match in one of the most peculiar sporting events of recent history. McGregor had grown up boxing but had never been in a professional boxing match before, and he was used to preparing for Mixed Martial Arts matches.

Even for an experienced championship boxer, fighting Mayweather would be a tough task. But to be a boxing debutant taking on Mayweather, that was almost unthinkable. Despite this, McGregor showed a lack of appreciation for new knowledge by keeping his MMA-coaches as his sole source of wisdom during the fight, and he paid severely for it.

McGregor began the fight better than most of the critics expected. But as Mayweather began breaking McGregor down in the middle rounds, the coaches in his corner could not do much to improve the situation. This was directly due to a lack of high-level boxing expertise. Each time McGregor would come back to the corner in between rounds, he failed to receive the technical advice that could have kept him in the fight.

After being knocked out in ten rounds, McGregor said that he felt he had outboxed Mayweather in the early rounds, but added that Mayweather could 'switch up game plans,' in a way that he had not anticipated. Unfortunately, because McGregor lacked an advisor who had a wealth of boxing experience, he was not afforded the luxury of being able to switch up his game in the same way.

If McGregor had given a high-level boxing coach a senior role on his team, he would have received vital guidance that could have influenced the fight. Instead, he chose to stubbornly stick to a team that had little relevant experience in the sport and was undoubtedly overwhelmed.

By the time that Floyd Mayweather fought Conor McGregor, he himself was a boxing master. He knew just as much, if not more, than his father and his uncle. However, even Floyd still needed a coach.

A coach can see things that you may miss, simply because they are watching from another viewpoint. They are not under pressure or getting punches launched at them, so they have more mental space to make logical decisions.

They are better positioned to see the direction that the bout is heading towards, and they can spot if you are slowly falling out of the game-plan. You will struggle to see this as easily, because you are focused on the battle in the present moment.

It is harder to focus on the next round or two, when you have to deal with an opponent trying to knock you out in the current round! All mentors you select should be judged on their ability to help you excel and their knack for putting together plans in the heat of battle.

The more experiences your coaches have been exposed to, the more knowledge there is to trickle down to you. And if they have an ability to help you make adjustments, it is more likely you will win. Selecting trainers based on sentiment or personal bias may satisfy your emotions, but this may be at the cost of your victory.

SCHOOL OF FIGHTING

Falling in Love With the Squared Circle

The values that Floyd Mayweather Jr.'s father installed in him would continue to shape his entire career. Even though boxing was forced onto Floyd, he would come to fall in love with the sport. That love would ignite a desire to be the best. The seriousness with which Mayweather approached his craft mirrored the seriousness of an aspiring doctor doing overtime for their medical degree.

For most, school is the place that defines the career they will pursue. In high school, Floyd would often daydream of the future success he would have in the ring. And when he was supposed to be doing his homework, Floyd would instead practice his autograph signature. He would tell his sisters that one day he would be "*as famous as the Jackson 5.*" For Floyd, his school was the boxing gym.

Floyd Jr. had boxing on his mind 24 /7. The itch to train followed his every move. Even later on in his career, Floyd never got out of shape, even when he was not in training camp. He would stay close to his usual fighting weight, never packing on pounds like so many other fighters do.

Discipline had been ingrained in him so deeply that he was able enjoy leisure activities while being in training camp without losing focus. His leisurely indulgence never got in the way of his training because he knew how to limit it. "*Boxing always came first,*" he said.

Traditionally, fighters are encouraged to go into training camp with a prisoner mindset: little contact with friends and family, no parties, no girlfriends, no going out, etc. And for most, this makes total sense as few can balance leisure activities with the duties of training.

Floyd was a part of that "few". His leisure time helped him to remain dedicated to his training year-round. Since he was a gym rat who trained multiple times a day, the risk of mental burnout was higher for him compared to other fighters. Being able to release that tension by hanging out with friends arguably helped to eradicate the monotony of training.

When asked about the early part of his career, Floyd stated that he would train and party. But what separated him from other fighters is that he would train again right after the party. In 2004, Floyd Mayweather defeated an opponent named DeMarcus "Chop Chop" Corley in a WBC light-welterweight title eliminator. Soon after that fight, Corley joined the Mayweather training camp as part of the entourage and helped Mayweather to prepare for matches as a sparring partner.

After being accepted into Mayweather's friendship group, Corley got to see Floyd's work ethic firsthand. Corley saw how dedicated Mayweather was to his craft, even when they were out having fun. When Mayweather and his friends would go to restaurants, nightclubs, or even strip clubs, Corley saw how Mayweather still had training on his mind.

In a documentary before one of Floyd's fights, Corley recalled being surprised by Floyd's training habits. He spoke of how Floyd would walk to the trunk of the car straight after a party, then pull out the training gear and with an astonished expression, Corley would say, *"But we just left the club! You want to go run right now?"* to which Floyd's response was, *"Come on, man, we gotta work!"*.

While most fighters require their coaches and advisors to push them in training camp, this was never the case for Floyd Mayweather. It was the other way around. Floyd Jr. would be the one pushing the limits of his team and training partners.

Floyd Mayweather's advisor and close friend Leonard Ellerbe was a member of the team who assisted Mayweather on his late-night running sessions, and he would also have to suffer the consequences of Floyd's disciplined ambition. It could be 3 a.m. and Floyd would call Leonard asking, *"Where are you at? Let's go train!"* Floyd was up for late-night/early morning runs. But he also would go to the fitness gym, eager to train maniacally. Training was no chore that he complained about. It was a luxurious opportunity to *"train while my opponent is sleeping."*

"Hard Work, Dedication!"

Floyd Mayweather was known for working hard. Those who were in his presence while he was in training camp got to receive the "Mayweather Experience." In 2007 he opened his own gym and it soon became a "thing to do" for people who were in town. It was their chance to see a living legend at work.

As he trained, he would often yell out his mantra: "Hard work! Dedication!" repeatedly as he pounded away at the heavy bag. It was his way of pushing himself. He had taken two words that didn't mean much when said by anyone else and injected a certain vibe into the phrase.

For Mayweather, those words represented the feeling that a champion should have when he is motivated. People felt it when they heard him say it. And that's why for years after Mayweather retired, young fighters continued to echo the phrase when they trained. Their desire has been to recapture the feeling that Mayweather had when he used those words to push himself.

At a technical level, those words "hard work" and "dedication" are the traits every ambitious person needs. Dedication is required to push yourself to the top. Without it, you will give up when challenges arise. It is the thing inside of you that helps you evolve into the best version of yourself. Hard work is the thing that all people agree is needed to attain success.

All fighters are told that hard work is a crucial component of success. The problem is that the phrase "hard work" is broad and can be easily misunderstood. How can one work hard? This is rarely specified it should be done. But Floyd Jr. was a great example of how it can be done. And there are three different modes of work that can be fine-tuned to crank up your work rate.

The 3 Modes of Training:

FREQUENCY:

"I train every day, I train every day, every day hard. I train at awkward times, it all depends on how I feel. I never get tired, never tired." – Floyd Mayweather

Frequency refers to the number of workouts that occur in the days of training camp. Floyd Mayweather Jr. was a fighter who would train multiple times in a day as long as he felt healthy enough to do so. He was never resistant to cutting leisure activities short to go and train, as DeMarcus Corley described earlier.

The number of times that Floyd trained in a week superseded that of his counterparts. From the time that he was a youngster, Floyd's love of boxing compelled him to work out every day of the week. Traditionally, many fighters opt to take Sundays off. However, Floyd couldn't stay away.

In 2006, in the years that he defeated champions Zab Judah and Carlos Baldomir, Floyd spoke of his gym habits: *"I'm always in the gym. After the fights [on Saturday], Sunday, we'll be in the gym shooting basketball. Cause that's what I love. I'm a gym rat."*

INTENSITY:

"They say when I come to the boxing gym, I train like I'm poor, like I haven't made one dime." – Floyd Mayweather

Intensity refers to the vigor with which you work out. Some workouts are done at high intensity. This could involve sprints or fiery sparring sessions. Although it feels good to work out with a passion that mirrors your ambition, it is not necessary to train at 100% intensity all the time. It is also wise to balance out your training camp with some low-intensity workouts.

Low-intensity workouts could include sessions where you focus on practicing technique, rather than building muscular strength. Or the workout intensity could be as low as using forearm grips while you go about your everyday activities. This was the case when Floyd Mayweather was on a television news network being interviewed in 2009 to announce his fight with Juan Manuel Marquez.

While being interviewed by the CBS reporter, he continuously squeezed forearm grips to strengthen his forearms muscles while fulfilling media duties. In this situation, he increased the duration of his physical progress, even when he wasn't at the gym by lowering the intensity of the workout.

DURATION:

Before fighting Arturo Gatti in one of the biggest fights of his life in 2005, Floyd spoke of his training habits: *"For this fight, we boxed 17 rounds, 15 rounds, 13 rounds [at a time]. We boxed 5, 6, sometimes we box 30 minutes [rounds] straight. [One] sparring partner gets out, another one gets in. We box 30 minutes, 40 minutes, 20 minutes straight."*

Duration refers to the length of time that you engage in physical progression. For example, a standard training session might be 2 hours long. However, by increasing the duration to 4 hours, you may get more out of your session, if needed.

Do not feel confined by the length of time that you previously set out to do. If you need more time to perfect a specific technique, then delay your post-workout activities if possible. Your progress is your priority. Imagine that you are training as hard as Floyd would. Better yet, how would you prepare if you were going to face him?

Floyd would push the duration of his workouts to such an extent that it seemed extreme. Even though a championship fight is 12 rounds long with 3-minute rounds, Floyd would often push himself well past these limits, which is one of the reasons that he never got tired in a match.

CHAMP-TIP: THE 40-ROUND WORKOUT

Floyd Mayweather Jr.'s Typical Training Session:

Reported by Jeff Mar (writer for boxingnewsandviews.com who watched Mayweather's open workout sessions for Canelo (2013) and the two Marcos Maidana matches (2014).

Round 1-3 (10 minutes): Shadowboxing

- Warm up into the workout
- Practice footwork and technique

Round 3-7 (15-18 minutes): Pad-work with Uncle Roger

- Based on speed and quick combination punching

Round 8-10 (10 minutes): Body pad with friend 'Big Nate'

- Practicing short jabs, short hooks directed at the mid-section

- Nate will pressure Mayweather by walking him down

Round 11-14 (12-15 minutes): Heavy bag

- Work on combination punching
- Focus on speed and proper technique

Round 15-18 (12-15 minutes): Pad-work again with Uncle Roger

- As well as combinations, Mayweather Jr. working on slips and weaves
- Roger and Floyd would carry out the workout mostly in silence, owed to the great chemistry the two

Round 19-21 (10 minutes): Body pad again

- Allowing Roger to catch a break, Mayweather continued his combination punching with Big Nate
- A great alternative for fighters who have no partner, who can wear the body pad, is to go on the heavy bag and throw body shots

Round 22-23 (6-8 minutes): Heavy bag

- Focus on endurance work
- Working on continuous double combinations (such as 1-2's, left-right hooks, right -left hooks)

Round 24-26 (10 minutes): Pad-work again with Uncle Roger

- Practice speed without breaking momentum and maintain form and technique

Round 27-29 (10 minutes): Speed-bag

- Work on speed

Round 30-31 (6-10 minutes): Jump-rope

- Intense skipping, including double jumps, crisscrossing etc.

Round 32 (3-5 minutes): Weighted jump-rope

- Skipping with 3-5 pound weights on the ankles

Round 33-35 (10 minutes): Weighted shadow-boxing

- Alternating between shadow-boxing holding 8, 5 and 3 pound weights
- Floyd would do 1-2 combos then alternate with periods of hook-uppercuts

Round 36-37 (6 minutes): Ab-workout

- 50 ab roll-outs and 200 sit-ups x 2

Round 38-39 (6 minutes): Weighted neck-exercises

- With 25 pound neck harness
- Raise 50 times with a short break
- Sets of 3-6

Round 40

- 50 push ups x 3 sets

Floyd would do this type of workout up to three times a day. This has been presented in the form of rounds but it must be noted that Mayweather was not limited to the concept of rounds. He didn't always work to a timer and could simply move onto the next workout without taking the usual one-minute break. These particular workouts also do not also take into account his sparring sessions.

Mayweather's road work/ running routine would range between 5-8 miles. And he often ran late at night (or early morning), at times such as 1am or 3.30am. And he was fit enough to run 5 minute miles.

Are You *Really* Working Hard?

The idea of outworking his opponent would energize Floyd. This is one of the reasons he chose to train in the early hours of the morning. Floyd knew that his opponents would not be working at those times. So he felt that he had his psychological edge as he could tell himself that he had sacrificed more than his opponent.

The most important take from this is that hard work is not just defined by how hard you think you are working. The value of your hard work is also determined by how hard you are working in relation to others.

If you are working hard by your standards, yet are still not working harder than everyone else, then your version of 'hard work' won't make a huge difference. But, if you are working harder than everyone else, then that is what will get you results.

Mayweather also exhibited this attitude by continuously staying in shape, even when he was not in fight camp. In contrast, many fighters neglect the gym and get out of shape when they are not in training camp.

Through Mayweather's decades of fighting, he continuously stayed in shape, and for every single professional fight, he trained hard. Many see his '96 Olympic loss (that got him the bronze medal) as the sole experience that pushed him to work harder.

Mayweather suffered a loss in the semi-finals of the Olympic tournament, though many believed the judges robbed him, since he had outboxed his opponent. Robbery or not, the loss pushed Mayweather to work harder. However, there was also another experience before this that taught him to be in shape for every fight.

In 1995, Mayweather was scheduled to fight one of the country's top amateur fighters, Carlos Navarro, in the US Pan-American trials. The match was set at 119-pounds. But according to his guardian at the time, Don Hale, Mayweather didn't take his weight management seriously.

On Wednesday morning, he needed to weigh in at the 119-pound limit. On the Sunday before the fight, his weight was 131 1/2 pounds, meaning he had to drop 12 pounds in three days. As Hale said, 'he had to get down real fast, and he did it the wrong way.'

Consequently, Floyd was weight-drained on fight day, and he didn't perform at his best. He ended up losing the match. But he learned a valuable lesson about staying in shape and managing weight.

Avoid Overtraining

Working your way up to a high training rate must be done gradually. Otherwise, you will risk damaging your body by not giving it time to catch up after it has been broken down. It is better to progress slowly, rather than to improve in quick spikes that are too harsh to maintain long term.

If you train at a high level in all three modes too early, it will come at the expense of your body's health. Though it is sometimes difficult for an ambitious athlete to accept, the body needs to recover from its battles. If you are training at a high level for an extended period, your body won't have the opportunity to repair itself. This will leave it in a vulnerable state, and this leads to overtraining.

Training too hard without adequate rest will cause your body to have little energy when you need to fight. This is known as "peaking too early." The body must have enough recovery before fight time arrives. As your body gets used to the intensity of your workouts, then the amount of recovery time needed will decrease.

If you are in the recovery phase when the match has come, you risk not being able to access the results that your training should have delivered. Floyd himself spoke of this after his 2012 fight with Miguel Cotto. Despite winning a 12-round decision against the Puerto-Rican legend, Floyd felt sluggish throughout. He was not able to be as evasive as he would've liked to have been.

In the long term, overtraining for years will cause your body to break down. This is different from the injuries that come from short-term overtraining, as these injuries will be chronic. Floyd suffered this from his frequent fighting schedule as an up-and-comer. From his teens up until the age of 30, Floyd spent this period constantly in fighting mode with little rest. His body paid the price, and he often went into fights while still nursing injuries.

On May 26th in 2001, Mayweather defended his WBC super featherweight title against a tough challenger named Carlos Hernandez. After winning a unanimous decision, Mayweather revealed in the post-fight interview that he came into the fight with "messed up hands" and had to take shots of Novocain (painkillers) to numb the pain.

During the sixth round of that fight, Mayweather damaged his knuckles after pounding continuously on his opponent's head. But he continued to fight the full 12 rounds, grimacing in pain each time he put pressure on his hands. After the fight, he showed his knuckles to the camera. His knuckles were so severely damaged that one of the knuckles appeared to be missing from his hand. This kind of thing was not a rare occurrence for Floyd.

A year later, on April 20th, 2002, Floyd Jr. moved up to the lightweight division (135 pounds) to fight Jose Luis Castillo for the WBC world title. Before the fight, Floyd tore his rotator cuff while hitting the heavy bag awkwardly. This injury is one that is well known for putting athletes on the sidelines. However, Floyd didn't call off the match as he told himself, *"I'm going to fight, because this opportunity may not come again in life."*

Floyd went on to win a close decision that warranted a rematch (which he would win dominantly without injury). Fighting with such injuries would force him to take a 2-year break from the sport from 2007–2009; as he said, *"My body needed to recover."* Had he not taken that 2-year break and continued to fight, then it is inevitable that he would have had a shorter overall career than he did in the end.

By understanding that there are three different modes of training, you can fine-tune them as your body requires. As an athlete, your body is your weapon. Like a samurai would sharpen and tend to his sword, you must do the same with your body.

On days when you have trained frequently and intensely, then it may be wise to turn down the duration of each workout. Alternatively, if you have prepared for a long time and with high intensity, then you can lengthen the time in between workouts.

If you wish to avoid the effects of overtraining, you must train with patience and care. Physical training involves breaking down the body and allowing it to regenerate itself. And, of course, when it regenerates, it will come back stronger than before. However, when the body doesn't have time to catch up, then continuing to break it down only weakens it.

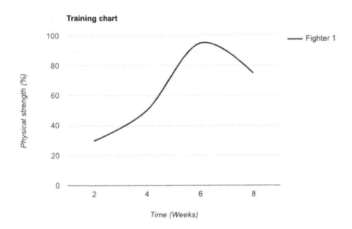

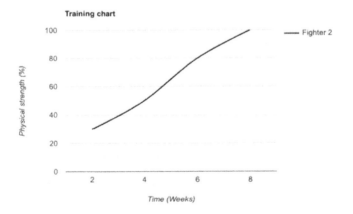

The two graphs represent the regeneration of the body under two different circumstances. The first graph represents a fighter who is training hard without taking time for proper recovery. The second graph represents a fighter who is training hard but takes breaks when needed.

The first fighter may get to a high point of physical strength quickly. However, he "peaks too early" and continues to work hard. This causes a dip in his energy by the time training camp finishes.

On the other hand, the second fighter works hard but also adjusts the modes of training to aid his recovery. He doesn't let his ego get in the way, he reads and responds to the needs of his body. Despite taking longer to reach the peak of his fitness, he gets to that point right before the fight, and he is less prone to fatigue when he steps into the ring.

A BELT DOESN'T MAKE A CHAMPION

It's Not Overconfidence, It's Belief

Floyd is involved in one of the great love stories in boxing ... with himself. It's a romance that is thrilling and moving to watch – Larry Merchant, 2006

In all of Mayweather's 50 pro fights, he was never significantly fatigued. This was down to Floyd's desire to push his limits in training. However, why is it that he could continuously push himself for decades while other fighters struggle to stay disciplined in one training camp?

One reason is the beliefs he held. It is one thing to believe in yourself, to think that you have the potential to do something. But it is another thing entirely to have a positive perspective about what type of person you are. Mayweather had both aspects down entirely.

Mayweather Jr. had shown that he was someone who felt comfortable believing in his importance and superiority. He is famous for his brash and "overconfident" character. Perhaps this could be considered distasteful and vulgar. But one thing is for sure; this "overconfidence" helped him to carve out a reality where the world responded to him like a winner.

Throughout his career, media outlets attacked his character, expressing outrage towards an athlete who dared to show such confidence. However, it is essential to point out that these attacks usually came from those that did not promote or live a life of success themselves.

They possessed a different mindset than that which Mayweather had. And on a deeper level, it may just be that their attacks were fueled by the desire to outlaw a mindset that was different to theirs.

A fighter who wants to get the same results that Mayweather got must understand the process Mayweather went through. Part of this process includes his mindset. This means that if you want to emulate his results, then you must also emulate at least some of the characteristics of his mentality.

Mayweather had little resistance to the idea that he was worthy of the best that life had to offer. He felt he was worthy of regularly winning, accumulating great wealth, and being a part of history. To uphold those standards, he was willing to do what was required, which meant sticking to the process of success, or risk losing the results that the process would generate.

As HBO Boxing's former commentator Jim Lampley put it, "*Floyd Mayweather is the most entitled fighter I know. Probably from somewhere along ten or twelve, he started thinking he'd be the best fighter in the world. He totally expected this*". At around the age of 16 years old, Floyd Mayweather Jr. got the first real piece of evidence that he had what it took to be great.

In his teens, Mayweather sparred with professional fighters. Some of these pros included elite fighters, such as Pernell Whitaker and Frankie Randall. By this time, Pernell Whitaker had been previously ranked the best fighter in the world and had won (and defended) the undisputed lightweight title and light-welterweight titles.

Pernell had superbly boxed the boxing deity Julio Cesar Chavez in a bout that many believed Pernell won. The judges seemed to be the only ones who thought otherwise, ruling the match to be a draw.

It was Frankie Randall though, who officially defeated the great Chavez, earning a split decision victory in his favor. This was Chavez's first loss after going 89–0. That adds some context to the caliber of the men who the 16-year old Mayweather was sparring with. Mayweather was able to hold his own, and on many occasions, even outbox these accomplished fighters.

Mayweather shared a good friendship with Frankie Randall. So out of respect for him, Mayweather sometimes held back so that he didn't upstage Randall in front of others. Floyd didn't want to ruin the friendship he had with Frankie. It was at this moment that Mayweather knew he would dominate the professional scene. The evidence was too strong for him to deny the beliefs about his quality.

Push Yourself To The Limit

In 2017, a criticism that Mayweather expressed of younger fighters was that many of them lacked the willingness to push themselves to their limits. Of course, many fighters want his results, but very few can follow the process. Even fewer are ever exposed to other people who share just a snippet of his type of discipline.

Thankfully, Mayweather was able to recreate an environment that could mimic the conditions that brought him to greatness. After opening his own his gym, *the Mayweather Boxing Club* in Las Vegas, it quickly became a place in which his "push yourself to the limit" motto was the guiding philosophy of all who passed through.

To this day, it remains a hub that attracts young fighters from all over the world who want to hone their skills. Fighters there could experience the vibe that made Mayweather great, and even more so when Mayweather would transform the gym into what's known as "the dog house."

'The dog house' is the name given to an event when the entire gym transforms from being a regular workout room to a mini fighting arena with the aura of a Roman colosseum. All the spectators and fighters stop what they are doing to gather around the ring and watch the current sparring session. Unlike regular sparring sessions, a 'dog house' sparring session is a fight to the finish.

When two fighters declare they want to fight in the dog house, they make their way towards the ring to the sound of spectators beating their fists on the rim of the ring. The raw drumming rings around the room, signaling the coming of war. Then, the timer is turned off, and a stopwatch is turned on to punctuate the start of a never-ending round.

In regular sparring sessions, the fighters spar for 3 minutes and take a 1-minute rest, just like in a real match. But in the dog house, the fight continues with no breaks and only stops when one fighter quits. The atmosphere is designed to trigger a sense of tension that the fighters would feel in a real match. The goal is to make the gym as intimidating as an actual match.

As Mayweather himself put it: *"In the dog house – sometimes we can box, what we call, 'till the death.' That means you fight until you quit … guys fight to the death. It's not right, but it's dog house rules"*. As distasteful as it may sound, it is an excellent example of Floyd Mayweather living by his motto of pushing the limits.

The energy of the dog house represents the spirit you must possess throughout your career. It is a fight to the finish, and it is essential to remember that your opponents are attempting to rob you of the chance to have your dream life. This is the perfect motivation to go through the pain of training.

It's difficult to remain disciplined through tough times, but when you begin to reflect on your positive self-perceptions, it helps you to stay strong. When a fighter pushes himself to the limit each time he fights, he gifts himself the opportunity to create the reality that he desires.

If you want the best possible outcome available to you, you must earn it. You must love yourself enough that you feel that you are worth it. It is this self-love, combined with the focused intention that most fighters lack. When times are hard, do not give in. Focus on what you feel you deserve and let that command you to continue on the path, despite the pain that it will take.

CHAMP TIP: PUSH THE LIMIT

After going to leisure events, such as parties, get-togethers or even media duties, Floyd would still go jogging or go to the gym late at night. He never let his social life interfere with his training regime.

See where you can push the limit and challenge your levels of discipline. After attending school, work or social events, go for a running session. While watching TV, do circuit workouts. Attend late night gym sessions. Double the hours spent at the gym and see how your body adjusts.

At one point or another, many champions make the mistake of becoming complacent. They stop training hard because they feel they do not need to be at full capacity to beat their next opponent, but as Mayweather said, he was always looking to train his hardest.

Mayweather's training attitude was dictated by himself, not the opponent he was facing. Few opponents were so big to him that they made him train harder than usual, because he was always training hard regardless of the opponent.

This is the standard that a champion must carry. Whether you act as a champion should not be due to anything outside of yourself. It is totally down to you. Your mind should be enveloped in the pursuit of your goal, even when you are taking time to recover. Even when you are enjoying leisure activities, it must be understood that this is directly helping you to recharge so you can train again. You should be itching to get back and train.

To prepare just enough to beat the opponent is never sufficient. This is not the behavior of a champion. You are making your opponent the center of your actions. This still applies even if you always get the victory. It isn't the victory that defines you as a true champion. Victory simply measures you as being better than the other man on the night.

It is the behavior of a champion that defines you as a champion at heart. When you stop acting like a champion, accept that you are no longer one, at least in those moments. This applies whether you have the championship belt or not. So then, it should make you uncomfortable to not behave as a champion would. With this mindset, it becomes easier to stay disciplined in training, no matter who the opponent is.

Doubt Avoidance

Floyd Mayweather Jr. was great at centering himself as the focal point in whatever was taking place, rather than seeing other people as influential in the results of what would happen. This served to limit unnecessary doubts in big matches and also allowed him to stay grounded in reality. Simply put - he would never give his opponent's abilities more credit than it deserved.

By limiting unnecessary anxiety before the match, he didn't let his mind make his opponent bigger than what they were. Mayweather didn't let the mental illusions that usually come before matches get a chance to create unnecessary doubts before the fighter gave him a reason to be doubtful inside of the ring.

We got the chance to see this mindset in full effect before his mega-fight with Oscar De La Hoya in 2007. Oscar was the A-side and the main attraction for the fight. After years of legendary battles, De La Hoya had far more experience in more significant events. For most fighters in Floyd Mayweather Jr.'s position, they would be prone to overthinking the magnitude of the event and undermining themselves.

Pre-fight anxiety doesn't necessarily mean that a fighter is scared of the opponent. Instead, it could point to a fear of what the event means to the fighter as a whole. In this state, the fighter becomes susceptible to the fantasies that fear creates. The aim is to remain grounded in reality. Being logical will give you more reason to feel confident, especially if you have prepared sufficiently.

Before the fight, in the pre-fight media tour, Floyd Mayweather was asked by ESPN commentator Brian Kenny, *"How do you think Oscar's power is, compared to other fighters you've faced?"* Mayweather immediately replied, "I don't know. Oscar hasn't hit me yet. But I know what I can do."

If the threat of punching power weren't enough, perhaps the fact that Floyd Mayweather's father could train De La Hoya for the fight would cause doubts. For the last six years before the match, Mayweather Sr. had been training Oscar for his other fights. And there was the potential scenario that Floyd's father might prepare Oscar for the fight, as long as Oscar was willing to pay the $2 million fee that Mayweather Sr. requested.

The threat was that Mayweather Sr. could potentially reveal some secrets to Oscar De La Hoya to use in the fight with his son. Oscar rejected the $2 million offer and chose Freddie Roach to train him instead. But it didn't matter to Floyd either way whether Roach or his father trained Oscar.

A reporter asked Mayweather if he feared the scenario of his father training De La Hoya for the fight. And Floyd was assured by the fact that no one could teach Oscar how to beat him since there would be no "blueprint" that they could use, since he had never taken a loss. Staying grounded in logic allowed him to keep fear at bay. Instead of focusing on fantastical reasons to feel fear, he remained firmly rooted in reality, which gave him a reason to stay confident.

Lastly, Oscar De La Hoya had built up a legendary reputation before this fight. The fans knew that on his best nights, he was capable of fighting like a fanatical beast. Oscar De La Hoya had been in there with the best, including champions like Pernell Whitaker, Felix Trinidad, Julio Cesar Chavez, Shane Mosley, and more. But Mayweather dismissed his legendary record, again remaining rooted in reality.

"You have to make me respect you. I don't respect what you've done with Pernell Whitaker," were Floyd's words. He instead chose to focus on the fact that he had sparred with Pernell Whitaker at the young age of 16 and had done well. And if he could do well at 16, while Oscar had struggled in adulthood when he fought Whitaker, then this was a good reason to feel confident.

Floyd Mayweather switched off any negative thought patterns that could put him in an unfavorable position. There was never a trait of the opponent that was so grand that it allowed Floyd to see them as superior. Mentally, he would never make them the "A-side." Therefore, unlike many others, there was never a time that he was mentally beaten before a match began.

Floyd didn't focus on the reasons why he should fear his opponent's advantages. Instead, if anyone should be puffed up, it would be him. So, rather than feeding the perception of his opponent's greatness, he would only look at the facts. Floyd made it clear that, on paper, he had been places that his opponent hadn't. Therefore, the opponent had more reason to have doubts than him.

Floyd was great at reframing the entire perception of any fight he was in, whether he was the A-side or the B-side, so that the reality was that his opponent felt as if Floyd was the A-side. If you did not know anything about the fighters before watching their pre-fight engagements and press conferences, you would usually assume that Floyd was the A-side purely because of his confidence.

To keep doubts at bay, you must remain strictly logical and grounded in reality. Do not allow the hype of the event or a particular fighter to skew your perception. As seen in his pre-fight interviews, when asked about his opponent, Mayweather would break down the reality of his opponent's abilities.

Floyd did this by factually assessing the opponent's career. He acknowledged their achievements and their positive traits, as well as their shortcomings. When going into battle against Carlos Baldomir in 2006, Mayweather Jr. was the challenger. Baldomir was the WBC welterweight champion and unbeaten for 8 years. Before the fight, some critics believed that the rugged brutality of Baldomir would present a stern test for Mayweather.

In the pre-fight press conference, Mayweather showed his ability to positively frame himself as the one to bet on. *"He is the official world champion, but I'm the best fighter in the world"*. With that approach, he gave credit to his opponent so that his opponent could not claim that Floyd was overlooking him. But then he also pointed out why that particular trait is still not enough.

Contrast this with Floyd's opponent in 2007, the Englishman Ricky Hatton, who was undefeated at the time. At the press conference, Hatton went up to speak on the mic. He seemed nervous and spoke in a much different tone than what was previously reported behind the scenes. It was reported before the conference that Hatton wanted to "slap" Mayweather when he saw him in real life.

Yet, his tone was extremely different at the press conference. Hatton seemed in awe, excessively complimenting Floyd Mayweather Jr.'s skills. Hatton went on to say that, at the start of his career, he never *"...believed that I could be a world champion, let alone win four titles in two weight divisions. The opportunity to fight the best pound-for-pound fighter in the world was something so far away from my wildest dreams."*

As respectfully humble as these words were, it certainly did not help win the battle of psychological warfare. And as Floyd put it, *"undefeated true champions don't speak like that"*. Floyd was the total opposite. He knew from his teens that he was destined to be the pound-for-pound world number one.

The aim is to talk like a winner, walk like a winner, and have your opponent feel that you expect to emerge as the winner. You should never give the impression that any part of you believes that you are not the better man. Subconsciously, you will allow your opponent to feel that they deserve the victory.

Like Mayweather, you can give credit to your opponent where it is due. This helps to avoid creating mental resistance in your opponent and delusion within yourself. However, you must state the reasons why you are the one to be feared. Once the opportunity comes, do not shy away from telling yourself why you are the better man.

Another benefit of making yourself the cause and not the effect of what happens is the ability to deal with hostile crowds. In June of 2005, Floyd Mayweather faced Arturo Gatti in Gatti's hometown of Atlantic City, which also meant facing the most hostile crowd of his career. Due to Mayweather's legal troubles, he had little time or power to negotiate many of the terms in his favor.

Floyd Mayweather knew the importance of this fight. Arturo was a fan-favorite, and he would allow Floyd to be on pay-per-view for the first time. Gatti had been in famous wars. Most notably, his trilogy with Irishman Micky Ward was one of the most thrilling fights boxing had ever seen.

Mayweather knew he had to make the fight happen. He conceded to Arturo's demands to make the fight in Arturo's hometown, knowing that the crowd would be extremely harsh towards him. Even the most tenacious champions would resist agreeing to fight on enemy turf. However, Mayweather didn't think it would make a difference, saying, *"I ain't worried about it. When it comes to the mental game, I'm the strongest."*

On fight night, Mayweather was right. The crowd's temper made no difference. He destroyed Gatti in 6 brutal rounds. Reflecting on the event afterward, Mayweather said:

"When I went to Atlantic City, all the fans were rooting for Gatti. For me, it's a great feeling, I felt good. Because I know, once we get in that squared circle, what I really, really know in my heart: The fans cannot fight for a fighter. It's just me and him in there. One on one."

The crowd should not affect you if you are mentally strong. The truth is that it really is all in your head. The idea that the location of a fight influences the outcome is an illusion, and Mayweather perfectly proved it.

Mayweather was able to focus on the only thing that mattered: him and his opponent. The most influential aspect of the outcome is the difference in skills. If the arena was empty and no one was watching or making any noise, what would be the outcome? If this outcome would then change because the crowd was going against you, it is due to how you perceive the crowd. It is a choice to allow the crowd to affect your psyche.

It is only the meaning of the crowd's hostility in your mind that makes you feel as if you are at a disadvantage. The crowd has no real effect on the fight, no matter the frequency of their cheers or boos. As Mayweather believed, a true champion can perform up to his greatest abilities regardless of the people's support for him, or lack of it.

It may be challenging to get in the ring and suddenly change how the crowd affects you. So this ability must be trained as early as possible so that one day it will no longer affect you. You must practice turning off the part of your mind that allows the crowd to influence your fighting.

The raw reality is that as a champion, the average person does not hold enough quality to be able to judge you. Being able to affect you emotionally is a luxury that should not be given to just anyone. It is a privilege that must be earned by those who hold significant value to you. The members of your coaching team and people who have proven their worth to you have earned that luxury.

Tactfully decide who has enough value to make judgments on you. Ask yourself, *'What have they done to show that their opinions are deserving of my mental energy?'*. Many athletes allow just about anyone to get into their heads. Instead, they should be filtering those criticisms and discarding them if they do not consider the source as worthy enough.

Now, if it were someone as experienced as Floyd Mayweather Jr. judging you, it may make more sense to give it greater credence. A critique from him will hold much more value to you than from a random person in the crowd, and understandably so. He may not be your designated coach. But because of what he has proven, he isn't just anyone. But if they are just anyone, then their opinion should be like a speck of dust lost in a desert - too small to be noticed.

CHAMP TIP: LIMIT VALIDATION

If Floyd Mayweather was affected by the crowd, his performances would have suffered for it. If you wish to develop this quality, remove your need for validation or admiration. Take a deep breath when you feel a strong emotional reaction and center yourself – whether the crowd is positive or negative.

Do not get overly pumped up by the crowd if they support you. Their support shouldn't affect your performance. This may come as a surprise as people believe that there is nothing wrong with being supported. But if their support has such an effect, then it also means that they are able to have the same effect if their attitude is negative.

CHAPTER 2: FIGHTING FUNDAMENTALS

QUOTES

Floyd on the foundation of his skills:

"Everything that he [my father] taught me from day one I still know… ..I beat all these fighters with everything that my dad taught me….. ..there are key things in boxing that fighters need. That's why I had the ups on most fighters. Because I had done those key things that my dad taught me."

"My dad taught me the shoulder roll. And I'm not talking about my dad, but I don't care who did it first, it's mine because I mastered it. Someone will say it's the 'Philly shell'… ..but at the end of the day that's the Mayweather defense."

"Boxing is an art where I don't have to be the strongest, I don't have to have the best footwork, but I got the best mind. Like I always say, it's chess. I know how to win."

"Whatever you do, even with guys that play football, when you guys are playing against a team that's not good, that's the way you practice certain things over and over and over again until you master it. So, how I learnt the shoulder-roll so good was, when I used to box guys that weren't that good, I used to box guys that were mediocre, I wasn't really worried about hitting him hard or hurting him. I just wanted to practice certain things."

"So if I practice the shoulder roll 100 times with guys that's not really that good. Once I get inside that squared circle with a guy that is good, it's going to work because I've already practiced it 100 times. Once again, they always say practice makes perfect. So what I do is practice over and over and over again....."

On a scientific approach to fighting:

"The fundamentals: everyone thinks boxing is [just] from the hands. The key to boxing first, before you even put your hands up, you must have your legs in a certain position. You must be on a pivot. So, the pivot is a key piece in boxing. There's a lot of details to boxing. You know, when you're catching certain shots, catch and shoot, a pull counter, an up-jab, a check hook. It's just different things."

"There are so many guys that got commentating jobs. But they can't talk about it. I mean, they don't [even] know about it. I can't say they can't talk about it, because they can't talk about something they don't know about it. So how are you a commentator?"

"No matter what no one says. No matter what the media says. No matter what the trainer says, when it all comes down to it, it comes down to the two competitors. And I know what I can do. One thing I can do is fight."

"Boxing is about skill. Speed brings power, but skills win fights."

"Everything in boxing and life is about inches and timing. And I think that's the good thing about me, I'm good at timing"

"You've got fighters who may hit harder than me. You got fighters that are very athletic. But you don't have a fighter that can make adjustments like me. You don't have fighters that can be on my level mentally."

"I'm a throwback fighter. It's really not about a weight class. It's about your skills. It's about who's smarter. It doesn't matter who's stronger, who hits harder, or who's faster. It's about who's smarter. When I approached the Zab Judah fight, people said 'well Zab Judah looked a lot faster than you. [But] I was using timing with Zab Judah."

"Some guys' game plan is 'we're going to rush him'. Okay, what's your second game plan? That's plan A, what's plan B? You have a plan A, you have a plan B, [and] if you don't have a plan B, then you go to plan C. I never beat a fighter with my A-game."

"You've gotta change styles. You don't want to be just one dimensional. Sometimes I may just squat low, just to touch a guy in his stomach. But then I may feint him [as if I'll punch to the stomach again] and come up with the hook [to the head]."

"I have more than just one style. If I have to bang, I can bang. But that's not my game plan. But if it comes down to that then I will bang."

"I use [my] body in my shots. That's why Gernando Hernandez quit... People say 'why did Hernandez quit?', 'it doesn't look like Mayweather punches hard'. If you're not in there you wouldn't know"

"I'm able to counterpunch. I'm able to sharp-shoot. I'm able to box and move. I'm able to counterpunch on the move. That's when you get a complete fighter and that's what I am, a complete fighter. When you say boxing, that's all you say is Floyd Mayweather."

"Everybody wants to knock everybody out. Once my body broke down, when my hands broke down, because boxing is wear and tear on the body, people seemed to forget I was a knockout artist…

I was fighting at 125 pounds in 96. A few months later, I moved to 130. From 130, eventually I went to 135. And I won a title at 30 and 35. I won the title at 40. I won a title at 47 and won a title at 54. And I never even weighed 154 pounds."

"Everybody's game plan is to come straight ahead, keep pressuring him [me]. Hit him on the hip, hit him with a low blow, head butt him. [But] I still find a way to win. They say 'this guy right here, he's super-fast,' [but] I still find a way to win. 'This guy's got a good left hook', 'this guy's got a good right hand', 'this guy goes to the body good', [but] I still find a way to win. Saturday [on fight night], I will find a way to win."

"Champions [are] supposed to adapt. This goes on in everyday life. You have to make adjustments. You could work a 9-to-5. You could work at a burger spot. If they say you're on cheeseburgers tonight but when you get there, then they say you're on fries, don't argue. Do what you gotta do. Just make adjustments. And all I did was make an adjustment."

"The thing is, whatever you do good, the best thing you do good, I don't care what fighter you are, I take that away from you."

"It's all collecting data. You see what he brings to the table. It all depends. My thing is this, I don't have to watch any footage of a fighter. Because I'm Floyd Mayweather, everybody gotta watch me."

"..before I face a fighter I size him up.. ..A lot of fighters show their hand."

On having high standards:

"The thing is I'm a lot older now, a lot wiser, a lot smarter. [I've] always been the type of individual that had an open mind. I don't know everything. I don't think I know everything."

"My crew like to watch it [my old fights]. So when they watch it, I like to look sometimes. And I'm a critic of myself because I always feel like I can get better. So any fight that I fought in, it wasn't good enough. It's never good enough. There's always room for growth."

"A lot of times, these coaches are inexperienced because they've never been put in that situation. I don't want no trainer in my corner when I'm fighting if he ain't never been in a fight before. You gotta have some type of experience in fighting."

On defense:

"If Floyd Mayweather was not a sharp, smart, defensive wizard, then I wouldn't have lasted so long in my career. And sometimes I sit back and ask myself, well where are the fighters from the 96 Olympic team? And where are the rest of the fighters from the 2000 team, 2004, 2008. Now, we're in 2011."

"If you look at Pretty Boy Floyd compared to Money Mayweather, they're two different fighters. Because when I was Pretty Boy Floyd, I was active, fighting all the time, every couple months. So I stay in the gym."

"I stay fighting, I stay in the flow. So I could throw punches, tear a motherfucker ass up. Then when I got older, you know, I stayed wise. I still continue to tear their ass up, but in a different way. But you got to stay in the flow."

"The last time I checked, this sport was called boxing, not toe-to-toe. The sport is called boxing. It's about being a business-man. If I'm punch drunk, can't nobody here pay my bills or look out for my family. So I take the least punishment but make the most in the sport today."

"This is not called slugging, this is not toe-to-toe. This is the sweet science. This is boxing. And no one has this sweet science like me. I make extraordinary fighters look ordinary. You guys build fighters up and say that these fighters are extraordinary and [that] these fighters are on my level. I just go out there and do my job. And guess what? It's never good enough [for the critics]."

"You're going to get hurt, whether you like it or not. And if you do get hit, you've got to be able to take it. Just like when Shane [Mosley] hit me. I bounced back like a true champion and did what I had to do."

In a media discussion with reporters before his 2005 fight with the popular Arturo Gatti, Mayweather went on a rant denouncing the straight-forward approach of his opponent:

"He can't match me. He doesn't move his head. His jab is not better than mine. His right hand's not better than mine. His left hook come[s] too wide. He bleed[s] easy. He can't take it to the body. He showed that he can go down from a head-shot or a body-shot. I haven't shown that yet."

"I haven't shown my weakness in boxing. So that's the difference. I'm going to take his belt. I ain't gonna defend it, I'ma give it right back. [We're] champion's right here. He can't beat me and I know it. I got the will to win. I know how to win. I'm a smarter fighter than he is."

"They talking about 'he's willing to die in there'. I ain't willing to die because I don't gotta die in there! I know I'm not. Because the less you get hit, the longer you last in the sport of boxing. Smart fighters always prevail. It's called longevity."

"He's a A-B-C, 1-2-3 [type of fighter]. You can sit there and try to depend on them big shots all you want to. While he's depending on them big shots, I'ma steady pile up points, steady rack up points. And before you know it, either his eyes gon' be closed, he's gonna bleed, I'ma put him out."

"You know me, I'm a smart fighter, intelligent boxer.. ...it's not cool.. ...It's not great to take punishment. Just 'cause you can bleed, it ain't cool to bleed!"

IT'S ABOUT 'SMARTS'

Boxing Is a Science

"Most guys I beat, I don't beat them with speed and power. I beat them with smarts." – Floyd Mayweather Jr.

Mayweather's work ethic explains perfectly why he had enough endurance to win all of his fights. But his mindset alone does not explain the importance of his technical magnificence. It merely shows us the attitude a fighter must have in training.

What ensured Floyd's success in the actual fight was his fighting intelligence. It was his understanding that the best advantage a fighter could have was the ability to deconstruct his opponent systematically. Though Floyd's success is not determined by any one thing (it is a collection of many "one things"), his intelligence was most responsible for his unbeaten record.

Theoretically, a fighter could train as hard as Floyd did, yet still suffer a loss. This is because training prepares the body, but it alone doesn't mean you can throw the perfect sequence of punches or make the defensive maneuvers that will stop your opponent.

It was Floyd's father who sowed the seeds that created the most intelligent fighter the sport has ever seen. Floyd Sr. instilled an appreciation for intelligence in his son. While many fighters take pride in their physical "advantages," Floyd was different.

This difference was clearly evident in the pre-fight press conferences, where each fighter would tell the media why they felt they had what it took to win. Each of Mayweather's opponent would focus on the following factors as their primary reason to feel confident ahead of the match:

- **Speed**: Quicker hands or the ability to move their legs very fast

- **Strength**: Punching power to knock Floyd out or the bodily strength to bully Floyd on the inside

- **Athleticism**: A body better suited to the rigors of boxing and legs that would give them better footwork than Floyd

Go back and listen to the pre-fight interviews of Floyd's opponents, and you are guaranteed to hear them talk of how they may be "*faster than him,*" or how they believe Floyd "*has never faced anyone as strong as me*".

These fighters lacked the understanding that all of those "*advantages*" could be overcome if the opponent can out think you. What is not as common to hear is a fighter proudly telling the world that "I am a smarter fighter than he is." This ability is what Floyd Mayweather was most proud of.

The Key Things

In Floyd Mayweather Jr.'s fighting apprenticeship taught by his father, there were many "key things" he was taught. And these "key things" provided a solid foundation for him to come out on top in all of his fights. Similarly, most fighters can achieve a good understanding of these "key things" by learning the fundamentals of fighting.

Many fighters (and coaches) describe the fundamentals as being "the jab" or other specific techniques that should be in a fighter's toolbox. However, this isn't necessarily the case. Specific actions such as the jab are just vehicles that help you to achieve the real fundamentals. So, what are the fundamentals?:

1. Balance – There are few moments in all of Floyd's fights where he allowed himself to be off-balance for an extended period. This is one of the reasons that he was tough to hit. His excellent control of balance allowed him to transition quickly between offense and defense.

2. Timing - The aim of great timing is to land the punch when the short, critical window is open. A great fighter must be able to capitalize on these openings consistently, and Floyd did this to near-perfection. It made him a great counterpuncher.

3. Control – Mayweather was very crafty. He did whatever it took to control the direction of the fight, even if he took him a couple of rounds to figure out how to do so. Floyd would control his opponent's individual body parts (such as their head or their gloves) to throw them off of their game, as well as generally controlling the momentum/pace of the fight.

4. Deception - Deception is usually the 'key thing' that is most responsible for creating decisive moments in a fight. By using deceptive maneuvers, you can attack the opponent without his knowledge (so he cannot prepare his

defense). Floyd was great at masking his intentions by setting up a certain expectation, then suddenly breaking from it.

5. Counter-fighting - Better than any other fighter in his generation, Floyd excelled in the area of counter-fighting. This is more than just simple counterpunching. It is the ability to find a response to *any* problem that your opponent presents, whether in the area of defense or offense.

6. Distance - Being the right distance from your opponent is what allows you to 'fight your type of fight'. Each fighter intends to be at the range that suits his physical measurements (such as the length of his arms and his height). The distance between the fighters dictates whether those measurements will be an advantage or a disadvantage, and this influences their game-plan.

7. Positioning - Positioning determines what type of punch is available at a specific time. A blow that could be effective when executed from one angle could be the cause of your downfall when thrown from another. Floyd was great at placing himself in positions that would make it hard for his opponent to hit him, while it was easy for him to hit his opponent.

In any contest, the better practitioner of the fundamentals will have a better chance of winning the fight. Though all tactics and techniques are simply tools that may help a fighter gain the advantage in each area.

ELITE LEVEL SKILL

There Is Always A Reason

When you watch a fight between an elite fighter and a good fighter, there is a clear disparity between their skill levels. If the good fighter does all he can, performing to the best of his abilities, he may still lose. This is down to the massive difference in skills. The elite fighter doesn't have to be at his best to beat the good fighter, even if the good fighter tries his best.

Often, when covering these specific fights, TV commentators miss the "key things" that make a difference. They will usually say that "there was nothing more he could have done," when speaking about the good fighter who lost. And this is because they lack the trained eye that is required to see the "key things." There is always more that could have been done if you are defeated. The question is, do you have the capability to do it?

Avoid this limiting thinking that there is "nothing more" you could have done. The fighter with more boxing IQ (combined with the physical capability to use it) is the surest person to win. Mayweather previously referred to himself as unbeatable.

No one in his generation pulled off the upset, and perhaps no one in history would have been able to. But this doesn't exactly mean that he was unbeatable. It's more the case that there was not a fighter who had what it took to beat him on fight night.

No fighter knew how to create and capitalize on openings with Mayweather. Inherently though, there are "weaknesses" in every style. Liken this to a medicinal drug with excellent benefits, but inevitable side-effects. There does not exist a medicine that doesn't come with at least some unwanted side effects. However, you simply choose the drug that is likely to alleviate the most symptoms with the least number of side-effects.

Understanding that there is always a reason why a punch lands will enhance your control over the outcome. Your task is to figure out why a fighter is able (or not able) to do certain things. Rather than just fighting for the sake of passionate expression, fight from a scientific angle.

If you take a step to the left, understand why you are doing so. If you punch at a certain angle, know consciously that this will give a particular result that would be different if thrown at another angle. And keep in mind the "key things."

For example, how will a particular punch affect your balance if you throw it from a particular position, and what can you do to account for this? Be intentional about every single action you take.

Prioritizing Defense

Floyd's father trained Mayweather up until young Floyd was 16 years old. At this time, Floyd Sr. was convicted to five years in prison on a drug charge, and that is when Uncle Roger took over. Mayweather Sr. resumed training Mayweather Jr. after he was released, right before Mayweather Jr. got his first title shot against the respected super-featherweight WBC champion Genaro Hernandez.

Floyd won the title at the tender age of 21 (becoming the youngest titleholder at the time and the first 96' Olympian to win a title). Floyd Sr. continued to train him until 2000 when their relationship began to disintegrate, and his uncle Roger took over once again. Immediately Roger had Floyd Jr. fighting a more offensive fight, though at the expense of defensive perfection.

Floyd's uncle Roger Mayweather was the brother who prioritized offense. "You don't win fights by being defensive. You win fights by punches landed," Roger Mayweather would say. It was Floyd Mayweather Sr. who instilled the necessity of defense in Floyd Jr. Between his father and uncle, Floyd was taught the best of both worlds. However, it was arguably Floyd's defensive foundation that made him unbeatable.

Even though great offense earns victories, it is an excellent defense that prevents the opponent from winning the fight. Points are scored by the number of punches a fighter can land. So the less he lands, the less he scores.

Take Mayweather's 2003 victory against Phillip Ndou. Ndou was a terrific power puncher from South Africa with a record of 31 wins and only 1 loss. Of those 31 wins, he had scored a remarkable number of 30 knockouts. In their match, the two fighters had very different approaches.

Mayweather prioritized accuracy. He threw 304 punches in the fight, yet he landed 158 of them (a 52% connect rate). Ndou was more aggressive, throwing 460 punches. However, Ndou landed only 92 of them (a 20% connect rate).

Despite Ndou throwing more punches, the defense of Mayweather prevented most of them from landing. As a result, Ndou only won one round before the fight was stopped in the seventh round, and this was down to great defense.

"... As Long As You Win"

In Mayweather's second career (after a 2-year hiatus from 2007 to 2009), every opponent he faced was an elite competitor. Yet despite the caliber of those fighters, Mayweather made them look like average fighters.

By outclassing his opponents, he limited the drama that fans love. Mayweather could have made the fights more exciting by sacrificing defense. However, the aim is to hit and not get hit, as the age-old saying goes.

Mayweather understood that boxing is about being the best boxer, not necessarily the best puncher. The more skills you have, the more likely you are to win. So the goal is to execute the most expertise in the fight while negating the opponent's ability to do the same.

However, fighters fall into the trap of wanting to be the bravest fighter with the most "machismo." From an emotional perspective, it makes sense that fighters feel this way. They want to earn the respect of the boxing world. However, from a strictly rational perspective, this doesn't make much sense if the primary goal is to win.

"It's not how you win; it's as long as you win" was a mantra that Floyd Mayweather lived and fought by. For Floyd, victory was his chief priority, even above the fans' desire for bloodshed. If winning is your ultimate goal, then this sentiment must be shared on some level.

The extent to which a fighter disagrees with this statement may be the same extent to which he is willing to risk losing. The willingness to lose comes from wanting to please an audience who are happy for you to take punishment. So remember, entertainment is their priority, not your victory and certainly not your health.

Aside from the assurance of victory, prioritizing the "not get hit" part of the "hit and not get hit" saying allowed Floyd to have a good run at the top for an extended period. His dad told him from a young age, "The less you get hit, the longer you'll last in the sport," and it indeed turned out to be true.

Mayweather's longevity is something that is partially overlooked because of the extremely high standard that he set in earlier years. Mayweather's first title challenge was in 1998. For the next 17 years, Mayweather's opponents consisted of either world champions, ex-champions, future world champions or world title challengers.

To win at such a high level for such an extended period is practically unheard of. The majority of athletes (in all sports) are lucky to have a 5-year run at the top of their game. So, to perform better than his competition for nearly two entire decades is incredible, especially considering that boxing is a young man's game.

Floyd Mayweather put his ability to have a long career down to "not taking punishment." From his perspective, there was nothing cool about accumulating punishment. Meanwhile, the widely held viewpoint in the boxing world is that battle scars come with honor.

What if, instead of valuing validation from your peers, you chose to value winning at the minimum cost? What if, instead of seeing a cut or a bruise as proof of your strength, you saw it as proof of your vulnerability? It will ensure that your opponent finds it difficult to win and it will also extend your career.

Boxing isn't necessarily about the best "toe-to-toe" warrior. If the goal is to "hit and not get hit," then by allowing yourself to take a punch so you can give one back is simply straying from what you are supposed to do. Prioritize defense as much as offense and begin to view great defensive tactics to be as cool as aggression.

Any apprehension to adopt this mindset may come from a fear of not entertaining the public. As boxing is a sport in which the most entertaining fighter will make the most money, this is a valid concern. But, when it comes down to it, the priority is to win, even if on some occasions it may not be as entertaining.

Any willingness to entertain should never come at the expense of victory. Because when you lose, no matter how entertaining you are, the fans will soon leave you for a winner. This does not mean to be offensively timid in your approach, because you'll still only "win fights by punches landed".

Remember that if you do not perform at your best offensively, you risk not scoring points. Be smart first though, before you are stupidly brave. Be offensively bold, but do so within the confines of calculated risk-taking, rather than thoughtless risk-taking. Ensure your victory first... then worry about entertaining.

If you are a fighter who wants to please the crowd, become good at combination-punching. Adopt the mindset of "hit, hit, hit and not get hit," as opposed to "get hit to land a hit." A fighter who doesn't allow the fight to be competitive by being defensively effective may kill the tension that will enable fans to be excited.

However, if that same fighter is tremendously aggressive and lands many combinations, he creates another type of curiosity. The fans go from wondering,

"Which of these two will win?" to "we know who will win, but how will he finish it off? Can he get the knockout?" This dynamic can still give the fans an experience worth remembering.

Prepare For Moments of Crisis

One vulnerability many fighters have is not being prepared for moments of crisis. High-performing athletes require a tremendous amount of belief in themselves to perform at the top of their game. For this reason, athletes refrain from letting losing scenarios enter their minds.

They seek to place positive imagery and visualize their triumphs in their head, and rightly so. The only issue is that this leads most fighters to underestimate the ability of their opponents because they do not want to view the opponent in a threatening perspective.

However, by not accepting your opponent's strengths, you will not be prepared for the challenging situations he could bring. This is evident when seeing how young fighters with a lack of "experience" deal with the first time that they are seriously hurt or knocked down. It is often the "experienced" fighters who have been through this challenge before who know how to deal with it.

Experienced fighters know that when you are staggered by a punch, you must clinch/hold and do what you can to negate your opponent's aggression. However, inexperienced fighters may try to continue throwing punches, and they often refrain from clinching.

It takes time to accept that it is smarter to forget the ego and hold the opponent until your senses come back. Why wait until you've suffered on the big stage (where it counts) to learn how to deal with the challenge?

A fighter usually trains in order to become proficient at taking advantage of good moments, but he should also learn how to turn unfortunate moments into good moments. Tough moments are sure to come, so rather than allowing yourself to be helpless when these times come, prepare for them.

This doesn't mean the challenge will come, and it doesn't mean that you become a pessimist and imagine that you will lose. What it does do is make you a realist, rather than an unrealistic optimist. You are preparing for every scenario that could happen, including the bad. The overly optimistic person will be ill-prepared for a bad moment, leaving himself at a disadvantage.

For example, while preparing for the opponent, keep in mind what he does well. Do not disregard his strengths, as this is a form of disrespect that you could pay for. Acknowledge any vulnerabilities you have that the opposing team will be trying to capitalize on. Be prepared for the event that you could be at a disadvantage.

Another scenario you could prepare for is when you are hurt and need to mask your pain. You may even want to practice how to get up from a knockdown in the best way you can. When the time comes that you are hurt, the referee (and the opponent) will be watching to see how you react.

By practicing for this moment, you'll be able to give the impression that you can continue fighting. The key takeaway here is this - preparing for moments of crisis is just as important as trying to create moments of triumph.

STYLES MAKE FIGHTS

Strengths and Weaknesses

In Mayweather's forty-nine fight career, he faced a range of different styles. From tough sluggers to slick boxers, and from uniquely awkward punchers to endlessly aggressive brawlers. Floyd Mayweather Jr. met them all. So, to retain his undefeated record, it required him to adopt different styles for each opponent he faced.

As they say, "styles make fights". Specifically, this refers to the chances of success that a particular style has when it is pitted against another style. Your style may work wonders against one style... but it may be your downfall when up against a different style.

Let's look at Mayweather's preferred style of fighting, the shoulder roll style:

The common high-held-guard stance:

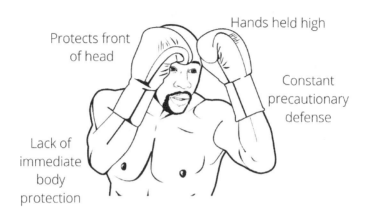

Hands held high

Protects front
of head

Constant
precautionary
defense

Lack of
immediate
body
protection

The 'Philly-Shell' Guard, adopted by Mayweather:

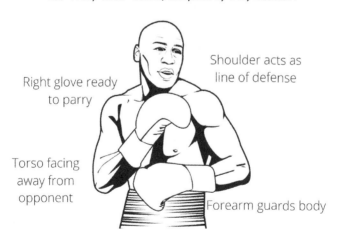

Shoulder acts as
line of defense

Right glove ready
to parry

Torso facing
away from
opponent

Forearm guards body

Mayweather's shoulder roll style was a defensive-based approach that was incredibly efficient in terms of energy expenditure. The general setup of the style involved the rear glove (right fist) being held high up to guard the right cheek.

The front arm (left side) meanwhile is held relatively low, with the forearm being held across the stomach so that it shields the mid-section. Though this seemed to leave the head unguarded on the left side, this was not necessarily the case.

Instead of using the left glove to guard the face, Floyd used his left shoulder to act as a line of defense. And while holding his arms in that way, he stood in a side-on stance, meaning that he stood perpendicular to the opponent, as opposed to directly facing his chest to his opponent.

In televised demonstrations with "In This Corner" and ESPN, Mayweather broke down the specifics of his approach, teaching the hosts James Smith and Brian Kenny that his style is inherently efficient. Each body part can defend multiple types of punches with little movement. And there were also numerous counterpunches available in the style, with minimal adjustment needed.

The highly-held right glove is great at defending a left hook. But it is also in place to defend a jab and right hand without needing to be moved much. If a jab came through, Mayweather could parry it (or swat it down). If a right cross came through, Mayweather could catch it with his right glove.

In a conventional high-held guard that many fighters use, both fists are held high to the cheeks, and the opponent stands parallel to the opponent. But this is not as adept at defending hooks, because a hook can land behind the gloves in this position.

In Mayweather's shoulder rolling style, the left side is guarded by the left shoulder and is also defensively plentiful. Then, by twisting at the waist over to the right, Mayweather instantly removed any potential targets from his opponent's reach.

The center of his body, including his head and torso, was moved out of sight. Thus, Mayweather had negated the use of all types of punches from the right side of his opponent (right-hand punches).

Due to the apparent openness of the style, Mayweather lured opponents in, encouraging them to come in with punches so that they fell within punching range. Because his left hand was held low, it naturally appeared that he was vulnerable. However, opponents would quickly find Mayweather's deceptive defense to be very stubborn.

For the opponent to find the target, it demanded extreme mental energy. Opponents were tasked with trying to attack, while also thinking about remaining defensively responsible. When they were preoccupied with trying to punch, they would often leave themselves vulnerable to receiving a counterpunch.

After throwing their weight forward in an attempt to reach the target, opponents would fall off balance and, as we previously discussed, being off-balance is a violation of the fundamentals of fighting.

Floyd Mayweather's shoulder rolling style was effective. But this does not mean that it didn't have its vulnerabilities too. Just like with any other style, it can be susceptible to the advantages of some particular fighting approaches.

For example, some of the fighters who achieved success in tackling it (be it relative) were aggressive brawlers who came forward and pressured Floyd. Take Luis Castillo and Marcos Maidana, the only two fighters who did enough to deserve a rematch against Mayweather.

In the rematches with Mayweather, both fighters were outclassed in a way that dwarfed their first performances. However, in their first attempts, they had success by pressuring Mayweather with relentless close-range activity and pounding him alongside the ropes of the ring. For a fighter like Floyd, who likes to be patient, the pressure of this relentless approach robbed Mayweather of the time to break his opponent down intelligently.

Another approach that worked well against Floyd was a well-timed right-hand punch, though it is a testament to Mayweather's stupendous defense that you could count the number of clean punches he took in his entire career on two hands! From the limited list of punches that ever significantly hurt Mayweather, many of those shots were overhand rights.

Since he held his left-hand low, the likeliest openings would naturally be on the left side of his head. Mayweather used his shoulder to block the right hand and, though it didn't take a lot of effort to lift his shoulder, it still required sustained focus.

With fighters who adopt a conventional high-held guard (with both fists held high to the head), there is still at least some protection always there. Even if the concentration dropped for a moment, the guard is up. However, with a guard that is held low like Mayweather's, the protection is dependent on his attention. Inevitably, as it is impossible to have total focus 100% of the time, the fighter will occasionally be vulnerable.

Adapting – Fight Smart Under Pressure

As effective as Floyd Mayweather's style was, there were inherent vulnerabilities. However, through strategic adjustments and tremendous focus, Floyd was extremely good at minimizing these.

Floyd knew that one style could not beat all, so he changed his approach according to what the opponent's weaknesses and strengths were so that he could overcome virtually any opponent. This approach required a mental fluidity that few fighters can achieve.

Interestingly, Floyd rarely watched footage of his opponent's fights, even if he knew little about them. Mayweather instead chose to let the present moment show him what to do when he got in the ring with them. He didn't want to allow any preconceived beliefs about what might happen interfere with his real-time analysis of the opponent's style on the night.

Floyd believed that the way his opponent fought another guy would not define how they would fight him. Instead, Mayweather studied his opponent in the ring and made a game-plan to defeat them on the spot, as they were on fight night. Beforehand, he may have had a general direction he wanted to take the bout in, but as for figuring out how to deal with specific challenges, he left that for the present moment.

Some people believe that the fact that "styles make fights" means that some fighters will always have an advantage over other fighters simply because of their style. However, Mayweather's adaptable fighting strategy is an inspirational example. He showed that you can win regardless of your fighting style, as long as you are willing to be fluid.

While some may give credit to the style itself, doing so discredits Mayweather's tremendous IQ. Mayweather's ability to make his style work for what he needed was why he was undefeated. His style alone, without the ring intelligence he possessed, wouldn't have been nearly as effective.

Even if you fight differently to Mayweather, the same thing can be done. The only reason that it seemed natural for Mayweather to perform at such a high level was the fact that he started training at such a young age. The fighting family that he came from allowed him to be pushed in the right direction at the right time.

For example, some may have seen Mayweather duck from a punch so quickly that it seemed as if *"he moved before he saw the punch coming,"* as fans and commentators have often said. Sure, to the untrained eye, it might have appeared as if Mayweather ducked before the punch was even on its way.

This is because most fighters duck from a punch when they see the fist or arm coming towards them, and most people only see this. However, the beginning of a punch is first signaled by the feet, as this prepares the body for the twisting motion of punching.

Fighters like Mayweather are described as fighting with "instinct" because they are used to seeing punches coming at them, based on the very first cue. So, what Mayweather would see first was the punch as it was being prepared to be thrown. Of course, knowing that a punch was on its way, he moved, and this was why it seemed to onlookers as though he would move before the punch was thrown.

This explains why spectators described Mayweather's reflexes as magical. However, this discredits the work that earned him that ability. Physical talent alone cannot take all the credit. Mayweather's natural reflexes may have been great, but it is the consistent practice over many years that best explains these talents.

So what can a fighter do to train in a way that earns them magical abilities like Mayweather's?:

Work Smart: Inside The Gym – The Cycle of Progress

The "cycle of progress" represents the continuous pattern in which an athlete learns new techniques. By training "smart," you can keep building on what you have already learned by making constant adjustments that lead to massive improvements. This is much better than simply doing the same thing over and over again, with no purpose or plan.

ATTEMPT → FEEDBACK → REFINE → MASTERY

Attempt:

As mentioned in chapter one, a significant benefit of having Floyd Sr. as a coach was that Floyd Sr. could teach Mayweather advanced techniques. Mayweather could try out strategies and techniques under proper guidance, which included the now-famous shoulder roll style.

The coach gives you new techniques to **attempt**. At first, you will struggle to execute them, but you must stay confident in your ability to one day have them mastered.

Instant feedback:

On seeing any improvement points, Mayweather Sr. corrected young Floyd so that he progressed steadily. The critical feedback Floyd Jr. received was from a credible source. As his father was coaching him, he had someone who was emotionally invested in making sure that he understood what was being taught at such a rapid pace.

When trying to implement new techniques, **instant feedback** must be given. The sooner, the better. Some fighters make the mistake of waiting too long to practice the adjustments they need to make, but the longer that a fighter waits, the higher the risk that he will forget critical points.

Refine:

Begin the **refinement** process as quickly as you can so that you retain all of the advice. If you are a dedicated fighter, you may even take physical notes (perhaps with a notepad or on your phone) in the gym so that you can look back at them. When refining your technique, be as physically involved as possible.

For instance, when Floyd Mayweather's entourage watched him on the heavy bag or shadow-boxing, some of the younger fighters in the gym watched Mayweather with focused eyes.

While this makes some sense, the body does not learn simply by watching. It learns best by doing. So in that scenario, they could've gone further by mimicking Floyd as they studied him, literally copying his moves as they shadow-boxed or hit the heavy bag.

This would've borne better results than trying to remember what he did so they could recreate it later. By doing this, they could have made any necessary refinements by looking back at Mayweather and then making adjustments.

Practice makes mastery:

Boxing is not just about building endurance or strength; it is also about building muscle memory. The body must get so used to performing specific actions to the point that the correct method is "saved" for future reference so thoroughly that it becomes automatic. This is muscle memory.

The only way to get to this point is by practicing the same action thousands of times. By doing this, your brain strengthens neural pathways (the mental links) which carry the information that allows you to execute these tasks. The stronger these links are, the less effort is required to execute that action. And the more you practice, the more those mental links are strengthened.

It may take days or even many months (or years) to **master** a particular technique. But this only means that the ability to do it was earned and that you will be one of the few that can do it.

Work Smart: Inside the Ring – Analyze & Capitalize

The following is a passage taken from FightHype.com's interview with Andre Berto, the opponent Floyd faced in 2015. Berto broke down what it was like to fight Mayweather:

> *I was just so surprised [that] at his age, you know, how alert he was. And he thinks defensive first, while all of us would think offensive, like "OK, OK, we got him." He always thinks defensive first. He's always ducking, ducking, ducking, ducking... ...and you see him looking at you [while he ducks]. So he kind of puts you in the place of "OK, if I keep swinging too much, I'm going to hang myself out there to get hit." Because he's seeing it ... he's seeing all this [movement]...*

> *...he'll look up at the clock four times in a round, move around and move around then look up at the clock ... grab you, tie you up, look up at the clock, then hit you two or three times, enough to win the round ... ...and*

between every round, I can see him. He'll look [at you] to see if you're breathing hard. He'll see if you're getting tired. I've never been in there with someone who was so observant. [He was] very observant of everything that was going on.

Be patient and study your target:

Every fighter has their vulnerabilities and they also have their strengths. It is up to you to find those traits. Focus on building up your ability to analyze your target without getting distracted or mentally draining yourself. At the start of the fight, you must look for immediate, continuous openings, but as the battle continues, you must begin to look for patterns and habits.

Vigorously capitalize:

Once opportunities have been observed, take advantage with great commitment. This is much better than throwing punches with no plan, blindly hoping for the best. This is why Floyd Mayweather was recorded as being the most accurate puncher since the creation of the punch-stat recording system CompuBox.

When observing instant openings, take them as they come. As for taking advantage of habits, you must train your ability to remember what your opponent has been doing for the last few rounds. It takes practice to do this under pressure. But with experience, it can be done.

Let's say that a habit of your opponent is to throw a double-jab every few moments. Perhaps the first jab is thrown while being defensively responsible. But, if when the second jab is thrown, he lets his guard drop, that is when you can land a counter.

Just as Floyd would do, it is possible to bait your opponent into traps with this information. For instance, you could encourage your opponent to throw the double jab, just so that you can set up a counterattack.

Expect change:

A boxing match is an extremely turbulent activity. One punch and one moment could change the match in an instant. If a fighter wishes to be great at adapting, he must accept that he may have to change at a moment's notice.

Go back to Floyd Mayweather Jr.'s clash with elite veteran "Sugar" Shane Mosley in 2010. After a decent start in the second round of that fight, Mayweather was rocked multiple times by thunderous right-hand crosses from Shane Mosley. Amazingly, this was arguably the first time that the boxing world had seen Mayweather take such hard, clean shots in a single round.

When those punches landed, Mayweather's legs buckled and it appeared as if he would surely go down. Going back to the corner after the horrendous experience, Mayweather calmly told his corner, "It's OK. We have 10 more rounds to go."

After coming back out to fight again, Floyd told Shane in the ring, "You'll have to kill me," if he wanted to win. Floyd kept this composure, fought patiently, and dominated the remaining 10 rounds and to win a 12-round unanimous decision.

If Mayweather did not mentally prepare for unexpected changes, he would not have been able to keep his composure. A fighter must expect that such times will come, so he doesn't suffer from shock. Expect changes to come so you can remain confident that you can ride them out.

CHAPTER 3: MASTERY OF MEDIA

QUOTES

Floyd in a 2004 press conference before his fight with DeMarcus Corley:

"I'm never gon' believe that Floyd Mayweather is not a PPV attraction. How would you know I'm not a PPV attraction till you put me out there? Put some money behind me and you'll see I'm a PPV attraction."

Floyd on entertaining fans:

"It takes more than just being able to fight."

"I just try to bring entertainment to the sport of boxing."

"A lot of times fighters think that it has something to do with 'because I can fight good'. You have to have a certain charisma about yourself, a certain look about yourself, that Pay-Per-View attraction. I know because I was a young kid and I had that same look."

"Certain fighters like Oscar De La Hoya had that look. Sugar Ray Leonard had that look. Mike Tyson had a look. Certain fighters have that look and charisma about them to become Pay-Per-View stars. And if anybody knows about who can become a Pay-Per-View star, you're talking to the king of Pay-Per-View."

"People don't understand; it takes a lot of work inside the ring but you gotta work double outside of the ring for a Pay-Per-View event."

"I was a black fighter being promoted just with the Hispanics. Whereas I wanted to be promoted in the…. Hispanics, Caucasians, the Blacks, worldwide. So spread the money out."

"We're all in the same business. But I got a different sales pitch. I don't think that every fighter has to talk trash or talk bad about his opponent to get to a certain level."

"We're always trying to do things in a classy way. As far as when sometimes people see 24/7 and they say 'Floyd is hood', 'wild' or whatever. No, Floyd Mayweather knows how to sell tickets. It's no different to any other business. Whatever business, when it comes to sports and entertainment, it's the sales business. We're salesmen.

On media attention:

"Is there ever such thing as going too far when promoting the fight?":

"Absolutely not... ...In battle rap, ya'll can get close up, say what y'all gotta say. We don't gotta touch each other in a disrespectful way, cause we get paid to do that. Now we're fucking up the money."

"Every action has a reaction. You may touch me in the wrong way. Now I react. Now we done fucked up all the money. So now it was a waste of money to promote this. And now we're not getting the big pay days that we do. Cause we've done fucked it up. So my thing is this, I'm not gonna go out there and fuck up the money. I can't do it."

After being asked about this appearances on Dancing With The Stars and WWE:

"I did that, but what you gotta realize is that I'm outside the box. So, I'm real. I take chances. That's how you build your fanbase. I take chances. I didn't mind going on Dancing With The Stars. I know who I am as a man. I didn't mind doing that. I didn't mind going on WWE.

You gotta realize, when I went on DWTS I picked up some M's [millions]. When I went on WWE I picked up some M's. So, I don't mind being outside the box and taking chances. Because at the end of the day, people know what I do for a living. I kick ass, that's what I do."

At a media meeting, surrounded by media reporters, Floyd told them that he uniquely appreciates all of them. And a reporter asks him 'even if we write mean stuff?'.

Floyd replied: "Ya'll gon' write what you wanna write. But if ya'll don't write my check, it doesn't matter what you write".

On appreciating positive and negative attention:

"When a guy says 'tonight I'm paying, I want to see Floyd Mayweather lose', keep paying. You get another guy saying 'I'm paying to see Mayweather win', keep paying. Love me or hate me, you're going to watch me."

"My fans come first. Well, I must put myself first. But my fans play a major part. You've got people that pay to see you win. You got people that pay to see you lose. They both are fans because they are both paying."

On personal brand success:

"Once we do our homework and we look at the numbers, Floyd didn't need Nike. I don't have anything against Nike.. .. [But] I've never needed a Nike check on my back because I feel like honestly, I never needed Nike or Hennessy to run me $100,000 in commercials. That still doesn't define greatness."

"I think I'm the only boxer that's a chameleon that can adapt to any environment or anything. Like, I stepped outside of boxing. I went to WWE, AT & T commercials, Dancing With The Stars, whatever it takes to keep my name out there, that's doing something positive, I love to do it."

"Once again there will never be another fighter on my level. Because you have to be able to go where I go mentally.. ..And it's hard for anybody to be on my level mentally. Because I think outside the box. That's why I'm always doing record-breaking numbers."

"I'm always doing record breaking things. That's why I was able to go on Dancing With The Stars and take chances, and go on WWE and steal fans from the WWE.. ...and to become a household name, to become a Pay-Per-View star, to become a mega superstar, to have the biggest deal in sports history. I've changed, not just the sport of boxing, but sports, period. Everyone is asking for a bigger contract. Everything has changed in sports."

THE FIGHT FOR ATTENTION

The Struggle For Stardom

The sporting events that have generated the most revenue have always been the ones that could reach mass audiences. And in modern sports history, it is often a boxer who becomes the highest-paid athlete across all sports. This is down to the buzz that some boxers can create. In simple terms, attention is what enables the fighter to sell tickets.

From early on in Mayweather's career, he demonstrated a solid understanding of this reality. However, it was not until after 2004, that he would display the charisma that would begin to make him a star. The methods he used can be applied to any athlete, regardless of who they are. It is an area that a fighter must master if he wishes to make the most money, gather the most support, and gain the exposure he craves.

To further display the importance of attention, we must go back in time to a point at which Mayweather was not known as the sport's golden ticket. Floyd Mayweather first became a world champion in 1998, and he also entered into the top ten pound-for-pound rankings that same year (according to The Ring Magazine). The next year in 1999, he was ranked number two behind the top boxer at the time, Roy Jones Jr.

However, at the time, it was fourth-rated fighter Oscar De La Hoya, who was the cash cow of the sport. Floyd Mayweather Jr. and Oscar De La Hoya were stablemates, both under the promotional company *Top Rank*. But it was De La Hoya who was getting paydays as high as $9 million for one fight in 1998. To put this into perspective, it was reported that Floyd Mayweather had been offered a $12.5 million in 1999 for up to 7 fights.

The disparity would lead to a controversial dispute between the television company HBO and Floyd Mayweather. Mayweather infamously labeled the contract "slave wages," feeling that his value was much more than his offer. HBO's executive at the time, Lou Dibella, disagreed. DiBella believed that the contract was fair and that Mayweather had an inflated perception of his value as a commodity.

Floyd Mayweather was calling for $3 million per fight, which would put him in the same league as the De La Hoyas and Roy Joneses. However, HBO called for patience, telling Mayweather that those contracts would come later down the line. Dibella stated that Mayweather was, "*A star in terms of ability but not in terms of popularity.*" But he said he would give Mayweather a chance to increase his earnings if Mayweather could prove him wrong.

As the story goes, Dibella offered a solution: they would walk down Times Square together, and if fans mobbed Mayweather, then the television network would reconsider their stance. They never did this, and HBO didn't budge.

However, they did offer Mayweather a slightly improved contract after he defeated Diego Corrales. Corrales, like Mayweather, was unbeaten and had a significant height advantage over Floyd. But Floyd was in top form, and he knocked Corrales down 5 times, en-route to a 10-round stoppage. HBO rewarded Mayweather with a $15-million-over-6-fights contract. Not precisely what Mayweather wanted, but it was a step in the right direction.

Attention is Value

Fighting is one thing. Branding and marketing are something else entirely. Boxing skill does not exactly translate into packed arenas. We may read about HBO's dealings with Floyd Mayweather Jr. as a youngster and think, *'Wow, what fools! How could they miss the potential of Floyd?'*. However, based on what HBO saw, it made logical sense at the time.

Up until after his fight with Arturo Gatti in 2005, Mayweather struggled to get matches made with the big-name fighters in his division. Floyd knew that beating famous fighters would make it easier to command bigger paydays.

So after his fights, Mayweather would call out fighters such as Prince Naseem Hamed, Joel Casamayor, Shane Mosley (back when Shane was ranked as the world's best fighter around 1999), etc. But as he said, "these guys say they want to fight, but then they don't ever wanna fight," and they were in no urgency to make the matchup happen.

Before Floyd became 'Money Mayweather', he was viewed as somewhat of a high risk-average reward type of opponent. Mayweather could not sell out arenas due to the lack of promotion from his promotional boss Bob Arum, so those well-known fighters opted against fighting him.

Floyd's story is an excellent example to upcoming fighters that mastering marketing is vital. It was the lack of pulling power that forced Mayweather into unleashing a persona that was controversial, purely so he could get the attention he needed. At the core of media marketing, it is attention that the fighter must seek, and he must do it well.

Attention is an asset. The fighter, his team, the television network, the promoter, the venue, and just about anyone else that is involved in the boxing match will all benefit from it. The more the fighter can drive continued awareness of his brand, the more opportunities he will have.

Note that when I refer to attention here, I am referring to the public interest that a fighter can generate from the fans for his upcoming matches. Do not confuse getting attention with being well-liked, as Floyd Mayweather's success has shown that attention can come in the form of hate too.

Attention is not about being liked. A fighter may be well-liked with a "respectable" image, and that respectable image could hinder the fighter's ability to be a successful attention-receiver. This is because when he must break the respectable image he has to spark more attention, he may struggle to do so. In a world where competition for attention is growing, controversy is sometimes required to get it.

Floyd Mayweather Jr. discovered that the task of generating interest is not a simple one. From the start of his career, Floyd showed the charisma that seemed to be inherited from the Mayweather gene pool. In his early fights, he showboated and played up to the crowd while he ducked and punched his outmatched opponents.

In one post-fight interview, the commentator brought it to his attention, telling Floyd that he *"wrangled the crowd a little bit."* Mayweather replied, "*Some guys you love, some guys you hate ... I'm a performer, and that's what sells tickets. I'm here to sell tickets".* Well said - in a single line, that sums up the goal of entertainment.

But even that was not enough for the young Mayweather to get the attention he wanted. It would take even more. If he were to compete with the likes of Oscar De La Hoya and Roy Jones, it would take more than just a few random showboating tactics here and there. It would require a brand that could be promoted in the sports world over and over again.

For a fighter, adopting a brand means being more than just a good puncher. It means creating a persona or a storyline. That persona must express specific characteristics that evoke an emotional response in the fans. The characteristics of your brand must be communicated consistently so that the public knows what to expect from you. Though the general character must be consistent, the different ways in which you express it must be unique, so it doesn't get boring.

As fans hear the message you stand for, they will relate to you or hate you for it. Both sides of this coin are good. You are not necessarily seeking either one of those two things; you are just seeking an emotional response that will provoke them to take action. That "action" you seek is the act of buying a ticket. Alternatively, you want the fans to at least share your message to more people who may purchase a ticket.

In contrast, Oscar De La Hoya had a sound foundation for launching his career. His gold-medal success in the Olympics, and the story of him fighting in memory of his mother who had passed away, instantly created a brand before he had even turned professional. When a fighter wins a gold medal, he is afforded the luxury of being a highly-respected representative of his country.

The difference is easily measurable. In Oscar's third pro fight, he was paid $50,000, compared to the $7,500 paid to Floyd in his third fight. A strong brand pays well.

On the emotional relevance scale, (see figure below) of hate-relate, a fighter representing his country will be on the far end of the "relate" side. Country representation evokes a positive emotional response that makes people want to support you. As Floyd Mayweather did not win a gold medal (he won bronze in '96), he had to take a different route.

Whether a fighter is on the "relate" side or "hate" side is of little importance, the goal is to be on the far end of either side of the scale for different demographics. The more emotion you incite in the fans, either positive or negative, the more they will engage with your brand.

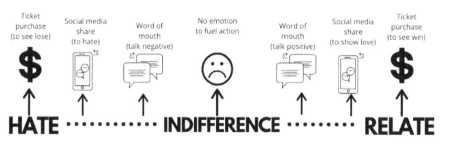

(The emotional relevance scale: representing the emotions that fuel action-taking in the fans)

In the early 2000s, Floyd Mayweather formed an image that was linked to that of an urban hip-hop artist, living a luxurious fast life with a braggadocios attitude. While this persona wouldn't exactly make you stand out if you were a hip-hop artist doing the same thing, in the boxing world, it would. This broke the typical stereotype of what was expected from a boxer.

Floyd Mayweather introduced his character and lifestyle to reporters with his slogan: *"lifestyle flashy, flamboyant."* He began to show off his fleet of luxurious cars and wads of cash. This would give the perfect reason for reporters to write about him and present him as a figure to be hated. It directly placed him at the end of the "hate" side of the emotional-relevance scale.

Even though this would rub some people the wrong way, it was certainly entertaining. Floyd Mayweather knew that whether he was liked or not, a polarizing negative persona would get more attention than a dull, likable character.

In a sport where each specific match needs to be promoted individually, the fighter needs to create anticipation. Even though Floyd chose the villainous route, it doesn't necessarily have to be the case with every other fighter.

There are different forms of entertainment a fighter can utilize. The following are examples of different storylines that you can build a persona to be entertaining:

- Underdog story – The inspirational fighter coming from nothing, fighting for a better life, and driven by the desire to escape from pain or poverty.

- <u>The champion at the top</u> – The successful champion who is proud to be at the top. His success actually alienates him from mass audiences who feel as though they cannot relate to his success. However, this fighter will carry an aura of "celebrity" that people will respect and look up to.

- <u>Representative</u> – The fighter who is fighting for a specific cause, which a particular target audience will look up to him for.

- <u>Humor</u> – The charismatic and fun fighter. The talking points of this fighter will be their unique humor, witty comebacks, or exaggerated acts of comedy that he brings to everyone around him.

- <u>Intimidation</u> – This fighter carries the intimidating energy that would be stereotypical of a boxing movie. Snarls, promises of knockouts, and a serious demeanor are attributes of a fighter who portrays himself as one of the 'baddest' men on the planet.

This list is not a definitive one, as there are different aspects of entertainment that aren't included. However, these five represent the bulk of what we have seen fighters do in the past to drive long-term attention successfully.

CHAMP TIP: TRASH-TALKING

Talk about what you will do in a metaphorical way. This creates a sound-bite or a quote that is easy for media outlets to share. This also makes it child-friendly and humorous at times.

For example, when Mayweather was discussing what a victory over De La Hoya would mean for his career, he described him as a delivery package that he would take care of: "I feel that I'm the best fighter ever. I already got the UPS box. With the Oscar De La Hoya [victory], all that's doing is putting the official stamp on it, and shipping the UPS box to upstate New York!".

The interviewer, Brian Kenny, was then in a state of laughter soon after.

Be Your Own Engine

As we have covered, the early years of Floyd Mayweather were met with a struggle for fame. It was no easy road. Critics in sports journalism and even executives at the television network believed he was simply not as marketable as he believed.

In 2005, when Mayweather was entering the ring to fight Henry Bruseles (who was the then-sparring partner of WBO super-lightweight champion Miguel Cotto), Larry Merchant stated that he could not recall a fighter who had made such a low impact on the public's imagination despite being at such a high level in the boxing world.

Merchant went on to highlight the lack of interest in the bout, saying: *"For whatever reasons, about 4,000 tickets were sold and not a single national writer is covering this event."*

It was clear that the persona of "Flamboyant Floyd" had yet to catch its break. Even more discouraging for Floyd was that his promotional team did not believe in his worth either. Bob Arum's (the head of Top Rank) main focus was Oscar De La Hoya, and fittingly for Bob, Oscar's image was one that was quite respectable. De La Hoya portrayed himself to be the clean-cut, nice guy, who most fans would find it hard to hate. De La Hoya had a persona that perfectly matched what society could promote as a role model.

Floyd Mayweather felt this image was not authentic, especially for himself. For example, when being media-trained by the promotional company, he was told to talk positively of his opponents, by displaying great respect and even admiration. However, Floyd not only felt this was "fake," but that a controversial rant would be much more entertaining.

Since this went against Top Rank's promotional philosophy, there was friction between Mayweather and the company. Floyd had many ideas about how he should be promoted, and he yearned to take a more influential role.

Mayweather told Arum that he would like to be promoted in different countries, rather than just the Latino community that naturally favored Oscar De La Hoya. Floyd wanted to be marketed to urban communities, knowing that those audiences would relate to him better.

He also believed that a boxer should be promoted with the same approach that a music entertainer would be, with flashiness and shock factor. But this did not resonate with Bob Arum, who wanted Floyd to have the Sugar Ray Leonard look, with a sweet smile and classy communication.

After nearly 9 years of professional fighting, Mayweather's PPV opportunity finally came against the beloved Arturo Gatti in 2005. Mayweather was the B-side in that fight, despite being recognized officially as the world's best pound for pound fighter. His mainstream appeal did not reflect his boxing prowess.

Leading up to the Gatti bout, former head of HBO Lou Dibella commented, "..his talent is astounding. But his recognition has not matched his talent. He can't sell tickets. Anyone who believes he's the A-side of this promotion is crazy. It's a Gatti event".

Mayweather perceived Lou Dibella's criticisms as an insult. "They put him in there against a C- fighter, and they have a war and a good fight", Mayweather said. It was clear that Mayweather felt that he should be the draw since he was the better fighter.

The media's apathy for Mayweather encouraged him to embrace the villain role. Mayweather taunted and verbally ripped into Gatti, calling Gatti a 'C+ fighter' who didn't deserve to be in the ring with him. In the end, it paid off, as the two fighters drew 300,000+ PPV buys, a great number for Mayweather's first appearance.

Still, the PPV appearance that would change everything for him was yet to come. After a relatively low-key victory against the respected southpaw Sharmba Mitchell, Mayweather targeted the welterweight championship.

In 2006, Mayweather fought on PPV twice, against Zab Judah and Carlos Baldomir. Beating Judah made him a four-weight world champion, as he picked up the vacant IBF welterweight title. However, Judah was coming off of a loss to Baldomir, who was the unified welterweight champion and had been unbeaten for 8 years. Mayweather had to defeat Baldomir if he wanted recognition as a legitimate four-weight world champion.

Mayweather had vacated the IBF strap before the Baldomir fight (in anticipation of a fight with De La Hoya) but became the WBC, IBA, and IBO welterweight champion after beating Baldomir via a decision.

However, those two championship bouts failed to break the 400,000 mark in PPV sales, even though he was adding historical achievements to his record. The general public was not familiar with a fighter like Baldomir, so it did not aid Mayweather's quest to become a superstar. Mayweather desperately needed to fight a competitor who already had the popularity that he wanted.

So the Gatti victory did not make him a household name, but it was the crucial first step. The next step was to take control of his destiny and separate himself from his promoter, Bob Arum, who ran Top Rank.

The long-term disagreements between fighter and promoter eventually caused the breakdown of their relationship. Floyd realized that he would have to "become my boss" so that he could have a pivotal role in his promotional direction. It would be a risk, but it would be one that offered him the chance to do things his way.

After defeating Zab Judah, Mayweather put up $750,000 to buy himself out of his Top Rank contract. And in the following year, the birth of Mayweather's most successful personal brand and persona "Money Mayweather" would be developed.

CHAMP TIP: COLLABORATE WITH NEW AUDIENCES

One of the quickest ways to grow your popularity is to expose yourself to the audiences which other brands have. It takes confidence, because it means opening up to audiences who are more likely to judge you. However, the pay-off is that you will reach people who you could not have by yourself.

This is what Mayweather did when he went on "Dancing With The Stars." A dancing show is not something you would expect a fighter to be on, but that is precisely the value of it. Mayweather was able to gain casual fans who most likely had no idea that he even existed before, despite him being a star in the boxing world.

BECOMING A SUPERSTAR

Tasting Stardom

Once Mayweather paid his way out of his contract, *"That's when we started doing record-breaking numbers,"* as he later put it. He formed his own promotional company, "Mayweather Promotions" under his leadership. With no restriction on what he could now do, Mayweather turned up the entertainment value.

The following year after breaking from Top Rank, Mayweather's persistence paid off when he signed a mega-fight with Oscar De La Hoya for May of 2007. Mayweather moved up in weight to fight for Oscar's WBC light-middleweight belt.

This would be the record-breaking fight that would finally offer him the chance to become a household name, and Mayweather knew it. He had been calling out De La Hoya since 2003. At this time, Mayweather was just a lightweight, and De La Hoya was campaigning four weight divisions above him (at light-middleweight), a massive difference.

As any master-marketer would do in his position, Mayweather made full use of the opportunity. From officially announcing the fight, up until walking into the ring for the match, Mayweather meticulously filled each moment of the event with high entertainment value.

Oscar De La Hoya was the perfect antagonist because he was already a big name and the two were vastly different characters. Not only that, but their fighting styles were vastly different. What added even more entertainment value, was that both men genuinely did not like each other, as they both believed that the other one was bad for the sport.

No doubt, Mayweather held some envy of Oscar because of the VIP treatment he received at Top Rank. But this was his chance to prove that they had bet on the wrong guy. From the first public promotional appearance for the fight, the games had begun. In one press conference to announce the contest, Floyd put on a spectacular Ali-esque performance to captivate the river of reporters where he engaged in an exciting display of psychological warfare.

After coming out to loud cheers, Mayweather and De La Hoya faced off in front of the frantic crowd, who were cheering at the top of their lungs. Traditional Mexican music played for Oscar De La Hoya, and Mayweather (who came out topless) flexed his chiseled muscles, beat his chest, and smiled to the multiple cameramen. They knew that they would be getting some of the finest content ever captured in sports.

Oscar looked on humorously and lifted his shirt to show his own set of chiseled abs. And then he turned and looked at Mayweather. Mayweather continued the hilarity by walking to the flashing cameras so that they could get a few more close up shots of his muscles. Before the speaking had even begun, this was an exciting press conference that those excited souls in the room would tell their friends about.

Everyone then sat down at the press table for the speeches. Fast-forwarding to after the formalities had been spoken on the mic, it was Floyd's turn to talk on the stand first. He began with the formal thank yous to God and to the people who had helped organize the event. And after those formalities, the real selling of the fight began.

The excited fans couldn't contain their screams, and a De La Hoya fan yelled, "Heart beats talent any day of the week!" It was proof of the exciting effect that this event was having. That heckling fan got Mayweather's attention among all the other fans, to whom he coolly replied, *"Thirty-seven opponents had heart. And all of them came up short."*. With that, Floyd's fans went crazy.

As Floyd continued to hype up the action that awaited on fight night, he also laid out many technical points that would psych out Oscar. He aimed to get Oscar emotionally frustrated. It was like watching an entertaining argument in the school playground that would have had the whole school huddled up in a huge crowd, watching a fight about to break out.

Mayweather went on to logically dissect Oscar's fight game, assessing his merits and vulnerabilities:

> *"Do I respect his fight game? Hell, no! I mean, I could've done the same thing to an old [Hector] Camacho. I could've done the same thing to an old Pernell [Whitaker]. I could've done the same thing to an old Julio [Cesar Chavez].*
>
> *I'm the type of fighter that beats the top fighters in my era, today. That's what I've done. I don't have to cry or complain. I don't say nothing. You put him in front of me and I'll beat him.*
>
> *It takes two to make a mega-fight. And he's a hell of a champion. And I'm a hell of a champion. And that's why we're making this fight. And it's more*

like this: He can have heart. He can hit harder than me. He can be faster than me. But there's no fighter out there that's mentally smarter than me.

Everybody they put in front of him, he's done what he had to do ... or vice versa ... Like I said before, he's straight up and down, no special effects. I can give it and I can take it."

Then all of a sudden, a fan interrupted to point out that Floyd had been rocked by some opponents in the past, to which Floyd replied:

"I got rocked by all 37, but they all came up short. And Oscar asked me, "Don't run, don't run like you did that fight." I tell him this and respond back with this: "If you could've run like me, you could've ran your victory to [Felix] Trinidad."

The crowd erupted in cheers and Floyd continued on:

"But it's OK. Floyd Mayweather is going to give it to you, raw and uncut. If you want the fake shit, here it is [as he points to Oscar]. And if you want the real shit, here it is [as he holds both arms out to present himself].

You can mark my words to this, whatever you want to bet, if you want to bet one million, if you want to bet two million, if you want to bet three million, we can. And I can stand toe-to-toe with you and beat you at your game.

Now get up here and tell the people what you gon' do! [Imitating Oscar in a feminine voice] "Hi, my name's Oscar De La Hoya. I'm going to do this, I'm gonna do that." [Switching his voice back to normal] You ain't gonna do shit!"

And as he walked off to sit down, he yelled to the crowd *"I love you!"*

The fans erupted in celebration of the rant that Floyd had gifted them. The applause was much deserved as the performance ignited a controversial start to the press campaign. It was clear that promoting this event would be easy.

The press conference mirrored Cassius Clay/Muhammad Ali's verbal assault of the then-champion Sonny Liston in 1964, prior to Cassius Clay's destruction of the feared heavyweight champ. And like Liston, De La Hoya could not match the verbal ability of his opponent.

As DLH walked up to the stand to, as Mayweather teased, *"tell the people what you gon' do,"* he paused before he turned to the mic and just stared at Mayweather with a frustrated face. His look seemed to say, *"I wish I could hit you right now!".*

Then Mayweather, not missing the opportunity to create more talking points, stood up. He leaned forward on the table and teasingly stared back at Oscar as if to say, *"I know you're pissed off right now, and I love it!"*

The two stars then proceeded to face off before the end of the presser. Mayweather's taunting gave the boxing world entertainment gold, and the fact that his antics were genuinely getting to Oscar made it even more interesting.

Though the fun did not stop there. It was time to take it to television so that the fans could get even more excited about the fight.

Controversy Sells

CHAMP TIP: BE A CHAMELEON

Develop the ability to adapt your communication style according to the different environments you are exposed to. This does not mean you should change your character, purpose, or goals. But it may mean adjusting your delivery, so it is easier to understand.

Floyd's communication would change slightly depending on the audience he was speaking to. For example, the way he would speak when on a CBS live news appearance would be different from if he was speaking on a women's show. And when talking to a female audience, it was different compared to when he did interviews with an urban channel.

For the first time in boxing history, there would be a television series that gave a closer look into the lives/story of each fighter while they were in training camp. The show televised on HBO was called "24/7," and it followed each fighter on their journey as they prepared for the fight.

Even though this would later become the norm in sports, in 2007, this was a groundbreaking advancement. Perhaps not at all surprising, the person who helped come up with the idea was Floyd Mayweather Jr. himself, who knew that this would be the perfect opportunity for him to display a character that would gain the awareness he craved.

Before this revolutionary show, fighters mostly communicated to boxing fans via the gatekeepers of the media (journalists, interviewers, reporters, etc.) who would then relay the message back to the consumers through the relevant media channels (newspapers, interviews, blogs, etc.). This show was revolutionary as it allowed the fighter to bypass the middle-men of the media and communicate directly to the fans sitting at home watching the television on a week-to-week basis.

Throughout the four-part show, Floyd Mayweather fully embraced the villain role, knowing that the controversy would create hype. The show bounced from Oscar to Floyd continuously, tracking their training progress and lifestyles.

In every segment that included Floyd, it was one that anyone watching could stop and ask, *'Who is that guy? He seems interesting!'*. Whether it was because you thought he was cool or you thought he was a fool, you would certainly want to see more.

Mayweather taunted Oscar throughout the show, bragged about his wealth, showed off his flashy lifestyle (including his $14 million home called "Big Boy Mansion"), danced and freestyled in the gym, and told fans about his lowly beginnings. It was in the run-up to this fight when Floyd Mayweather first announced himself as "Money Mayweather."

In one particular segment of the show, Mayweather flashed a stack of cash to the camera and threw one bill at a time into the camera while repeatedly singing his chorus: *"My name is Floyd, my name is Floyd, my name is Floyd "Money" Mayweather."* He sang that melody until he had used up all his remaining bills.

This was an effective way of having people remember his name, as opposed to if he would have looked into the camera with nothing but a monotone voice saying, *"Hi, my name is Floyd."* The HBO show was a beautiful display of opposing personalities that would gather many "relaters" and "haters."

In addition to the show, Mayweather gave fans some talking points right up until the fight itself. For his ring walk, Floyd decided to come in with a Mexican outfit. He rocked the Mexican colors on his shorts and wore a sombrero into the ring. He was taunting his Mexican-American foe and the pro-Oscar crowd, giving Oscar even more reasons to be frustrated.

Mayweather proceeded to take full advantage of his chance on the big stage, defeating Oscar De La Hoya by a unanimous points-win to become the new champion. After 37 fights and nearly a decade of undefeated fighting, Mayweather had reached the point that would finally give him the fame that he craved. The Oscar De La Hoya match would be the last time that he was the "B-side" - the tide had finally turned in his favor.

The fight was a box office hit. The contest generated $130 million in revenue, breaking all previous records. The tickets to the match sold out in 3 hours when they went on sale on January 27, 2007. The live gate accumulated around $18.4 million, breaking the previous record of $16.9 million from the Holyfield and Tyson rematch in 1997.

The event broke the record of most pay-per-view buys for a boxing match, reaching 2.4 million. Mayweather made $25 million, and Oscar De La Hoya took the lion's share of $52 million (career-high paydays for both).

After the mega-fight with Oscar, there was a desire from the hardcore boxing fans to see Mayweather fight up-and-coming champions like Miguel Cotto or Paul Williams. However, Mayweather's goal was to secure another fight that would have mainstream appeal. Fighting those champions would put him back in the same position he was in before he fought Oscar, earning respectable wins but no glory.

Miguel Cotto, the WBA welterweight champion, was respected in the boxing world, but was not a superstar that casual fans gave significant attention. Additionally, Cotto was still under the now-rival promotional company Top Rank, and it was difficult to do business with his former boss. So that particular fight was not made.

However, the two fought in 2012, after Cotto had left Top Rank. Their bout drew 1.5+ million PPV sales. This was because both their brands had grown significantly, compared to half a decade ago. Mayweather defeated Cotto via unanimous decision, and it was one of the toughest fights of his career.

As for Paul Williams, he was a tall, dangerous fighter, and many boxing fans wondered if his physical stature would trouble Mayweather. The issue was that Mayweather stood to gain nothing from such a fight.

Although Williams had just become the WBO welterweight champion after defeating Antonio Margarito, he only had one other notable win on his record (against Sharmba Mitchell, who Mayweather had knocked out in 2005). Fighting Williams would get Mayweather another title, but nothing more.

Mayweather felt that, by now, he had already proven that he could fight and beat those type of challenges. However, his goal was to engage in matches that would earn him the big paydays that alluded him for over a decade. So with that in mind, Mayweather chose to fight Englishman Ricky Hatton in December of 2007.

Ricky Hatton was the WBC (and IBO) super-lightweight champion and he moved up, from 140 pounds, to fight Mayweather at the welterweight limit of 147 pounds. Though boxing critics would argue that the best-fighter-in-the-world should not have been fighting a 'smaller man', their suggested alternatives would not have served Mayweather's purposes.

Hatton was the perfect selection for Mayweather because his home-country (United Kingdom) ferociously supported him. Mayweather knew that Hatton had 'a country behind him', and he was absolutely right.

In fact, around 30,000 loyal UK fans made the trip to Las Vegas to take over the town and support Hatton. They created an electrifying atmosphere on fight night, continuously chanting in celebration of their representative.

HBO-commentator Jim Lampley perfectly summed up the vibe of the arena before the fight took place: "It's an amazing scene ladies and gentlemen, unique in our experience of the sport, very much like being at a massive college football rivalry game [like] Harvard-Yale perhaps, Wabash-Depauw, Michigan-Ohio state. Take your pick."

In the weeks leading up to the fight, Mayweather took advantage of the attention, bringing out his charismatic side once again. When the second series of "24/7" aired, the "Money Mayweather" persona was in full effect. And even while in training for the fight, he participated in the show "*Dancing With The Stars*" to gain even more exposure.

The fight sold around 850,000 pay-per-view buys in the USA, punctuating a great pre-fight build-up. Mayweather's ability to market the event highlighted an incredible development in his career. He had now officially grown into the cash-cow of the sport. Fans were not tuning in because Mayweather was *facing* a star, as they did when he fought Oscar De La Hoya. Now, Mayweather *was* the star himself.

Floyd defeated the brave Ricky Hatton by stoppage after 10 rounds, putting on an impressive show in front of a huge global audience for the second time. Soon after though, Floyd announced his retirement from the sport, saying that *"I've accomplished all I've wanted to accomplishment.. there's nothing left to prove"*.

Mayweather's break from the sport did not stop the momentum of his brand building. He made televised appearances on the world-famous WWE wrestling organization to gain further exposure. Just like "Dancing With The Stars," this show was wildly popular, and although a WWE appearance could be expected for a combat athlete, an appearance on DWTS certainly would not have been.

By doing such appearances (including commercials and mainstream event appearances), Floyd was able to gain massive exposure. These appearances were strategic moves that would undoubtedly benefit Mayweather later, when he cut short his 'retirement'.

On May 2nd of 2009, Mayweather announced that he was coming back to fight the number two pound-for-pound fighter Juan Manuel Marquez on July 18. It was in this half of Mayweather's career that he truly transformed into something that no sport had ever seen before. He was about to reap the benefits of building a brand and marketing it his way.

Fight No.	Opponent	Paid attendance	PPV Sales (million)
40	Juan Manuel Marquez	$6,811,300	1.1
41	Shane Mosley	$11,032,100	1.4
42	Victor Ortiz	$9,000,000	1.25
43	Miguel Cotto	$12,000,150	1.5
44	Robert Guerrero	$9.922,350	1+
45	Saul 'Canelo' Alvarez	$20,003,150	2.2
46	Marcos Maidana	$15,024,400	0.9
47	Marcos Maidana 2	$14,899,150	0.9
48	Manny Pacquiao	$72,198,500	4.6
49	Andre Berto	$10,062,500	0.4-0.5
50	Conor McGregor	$55,414,865	4.3

TAKING IT TO THE NEXT LEVEL

Be the Main Event

CHAMP TIP: SHOW A LIFESTYLE

Just like with personalities, fans connect to a lifestyle that is being shown. People like watching lifestyles for different reasons. It may be that they want to vicariously live through you or they may use it to inspire them to attain a similar lifestyle.

Mayweather's luxurious lifestyle was well documented. Prior to 2013, he had based his pre-fight previews on boxing-related content. However, when Mayweather signed with Showtime Sports he began to focus on lifestyle content. This allowed people who were not boxing fans to relate to the pre-fight docu-series "All Access".

When the sport's most famous promoters, such as Tex Rickard and Don King, revolutionized the boxing game, it had always come after they'd made the sport more of an official event. For example, in the early twentieth century, boxing was a sport that lacked glamour and glitz.

It was likened to ballroom brawling, just for drunk men from the lower classes. It lacked classiness, and the environments that the fights took place in were usually dirty and not well taken care of.

Tex Rickard, who was Jack Dempsey's (the heavyweight champion of the 20s) promoter, helped revolutionize the sport. He made the sport more of a classy event, which high-class citizens and women could attend. Of course, giving the sport a credible vibe helped the sport to increase its revenue potential and mainstream appeal.

The process of making boxing an "event" that casual audiences could take an interest in is the same thing that Floyd Mayweather did. His matches were not for just boxing fans, they were designed to appeal to casual audiences as well.

These casual fans are the fans who just like to see entertainment and will tune in to a fight if it seems interesting enough, and Floyd helped to make the sport appeal to them by making it trendy.

The act of making each fight an *"event that you can't miss"* is what keeps the fans coming back. It is a part of the long-term branding process that takes fights to the next level. All fighters should adopt this approach if they wish to make casual fans feel as though they should ditch their usual plans to watch their fight.

As an entertainer, you must create a fear of missing out for those fans. There has to be a sense of urgency that will prompt them to take action (and buy a ticket) without delay. There are several ways in which this can be done:

1. Social proof

Firstly, the more a person feels that many other people are interested in the event, the more they won't want to miss it themselves. If they feel as though the rest of their culture (or at least their friendship group) is going to watch the fight, they will feel left out if they don't.

Secondly, if fans feel as though reputable companies are taking an interest in the event, they assume that the event itself is also reputable.

For example, before the DLH fight, Mayweather was asked by a reporter, "Why should fans buy this fight?"

Mayweather replied:

> Number one, you're getting the best fighter in the world. Number two, it's at the best hotel in the world, the MGM Grand. Number three, the best network in the world, which is HBO. But this is pay-per-view, so buy this fight. Number four, you're getting the second best fighter in the world, which is the Golden Girl ... I mean ... excuse me, the Golden Boy, Oscar De La Hoya. And the best promoter in the world, Mayweather Promotions.

In the April 2007 issue of *The Ring* Magazine, Oscar De La Hoya was not even rated in the top ten of the pound-for-pound rankings despite Mayweather referring to him as number two, and at that time, Mayweather Promotions was barely a year old.

Going further, it was Oscar's company '*Golden Boy Promotions*' who were the primary promoters of the bout. However, the fans do not focus on such small details when they listen to a fighter promote a fight though, and this is doubly true for casual fans.

Mayweather repeatedly used the word "best", and by throwing this word in a bunch of times, he made it more appealing to the ears of casual fans. It gave the event an aura of luxury and exclusivity. It stamped the event as something official.

It made the event something that fans felt comfortable talking to their friends about because it was an event that was of the highest standards. The event was something that they wanted to be a part of. If you must exaggerate a little when promoting, then so be it. It certainly paid off for Floyd.

2. Two sides

As we have said, a fighter's brand represents a purpose or specific characteristics. The more divisive the two fighters are, the more the fans can take sides and become emotionally invested in who they want to win. For example, Floyd Mayweather embraced the villain role to turn the people who disliked him into paying fans.

By embracing the villain role, this encouraged his opposers to want to support his opponent instead. Even if they had never heard of his opponent, they would just support them so that they could see Mayweather lose. This capitalizes on the people who know about the event but are not invested enough to purchase a ticket or pay-per-view.

You do not necessarily have to be the villain yourself. The alternative is to be the hero and make your opponent seem like the villain. You can do this through subtle suggestions, like implying that your opponent has villainous traits. Or you can do it explicitly, by directly pointing it out.

However, the explicit route should only be done if the evidence you have (that they are villainous) is strong enough to get people on your side. Otherwise, it can backfire.

Floyd did this himself when he villainized Oscar to the reporters in the lead-up to their bout. At a table amongst reporters, Floyd viciously attacked Oscar's 'unappreciative' character. He went on to describe how badly his team was being treated by Oscar's company behind the scenes, he told the reporters how much he loved them and how much Oscar didn't, as he tried to get the reporters on his side.

He also went on to tell a story of how after he had tipped 3 drivers $100 bills each, the drivers were shocked because they had previously had to share one $20 tip from Oscar between the three of them. They expected Floyd to do the same. Though he played the villain to the paying fans, he played the hero to the writers and reporters.

3. Competitiveness (intrigue)

As Mayweather himself said, *"I don't want to see no fight where I know a fighter will beat the other fighter."* It is about allowing the fans to feel the tension that comes with wondering, *'Who will win this?'* If the fans know who will win, this can take away some of the excitement. It is like watching a movie when you already know the ending. It is much more exciting when you do not know.

Mayweather usually took care of this by talking up his opponent's merits, yet without implying that they were better than him. When asked once if Oscar De La Hoya would be the best fighter he'd faced, Mayweather said, "*Yes.*" But even if Oscar wasn't, he claimed he would still have said yes "*because it's about selling*

PPV. It's about doing numbers". To the fans, your opponent must always be someone who is going to challenge you.

4. Promise of drama

Fans watch fights to be excited. They do not watch them to remain logical or calm. They want to scream, yell, and cry. They want to experience a range of emotions that take them out of the monotony of everyday life.

Fans must feel that drama is guaranteed, and this is why fighters like to promise knockouts, but this doesn't have to be the only promise. A promise of drama could be made by telling the fans that you "*have a trick up my sleeve*" or any statement that provokes curiosity. It just needs to get them thinking, '*What is going to happen?'.*

5. Call to action

The event of boxing is a product in itself. The aim of this is to bottle up the event as an experience and sell tickets or pay-per-view subscriptions to access it. The fans must be encouraged along this process by you directly telling them to purchase. If you make them feel that they will get entertainment value in return, they will feel invested enough to spend money.

Like all effective marketers, Mayweather put great emphasis on a strong "call-to-action," explicitly telling people that they must buy the fight. At the end of interviews, Mayweather was not afraid to tell the fans to buy tickets and tune in.

For those who attended the match, Mayweather offered "upsells" that the fans could also purchase.

Mayweather directly urged the fans to purchase merchandise because each fight was "part of history." For those who could not attend the match, he offered a "down-sell" by urging the fans to, at least, buy the PPV subscription. Doing this made sure that he maximized the purchasing value of any potentially interested fan.

CHAMP TIP: PRACTICE A CALL-TO-ACTION

The end goal is to make a sale. Mayweather was not shy to close the deal. As a profitable fighter, you must become good at "closing" potential sales. Practice your speaking skills and get in the habit of encouraging people to attend your events. However, you must always seek to give value first. Get them excited about it *first*.

Practice speaking with energy. Talk with animated body language and changes in your tonality. Practice speaking into a camera. Get in the habit of ending your speeches with a descriptive call-to-action.

For example, when selling the Oscar De La Hoya fight on an ESPN broadcast with Brian Kenny, Mayweather ended the interview by saying: "Two living legends fighting: Oscar, the Golden Boy. He's going to give his A-game, I'm gonna give my A-game. Blood, sweat and tears! Like I said before, it's going to be a toe-to-toe battle. So don't miss this fight!"

Being descriptive is more interesting than just saying, "It's going to be great, don't miss the fight!". Give an intriguing description of what's to come.

CHAPTER 4: BILLIONAIRE BUSINESS

QUOTES

On having a business mindset:

"I've set the model of showing fighters how they should conduct their business."

"For years, people said I was crazy when I told them I will be the first fighter to make 100 million or $200 million in one night. They said I was crazy."

"It's all about working smarter, not harder. I'm gonna get a check regardless. When I wear Hublot on my trunks, they cut me a check for 8 million.....a lot of people settle for less, I'm gonna get what I have to get, I'm gon' get it. I have to."

"You only got one life to live. So I'm not gonna ask you for anything, I'm gonna tell you what you're going to have to give me. You don't even have to shoot a number at me because I'm gonna shoot a crazy number at you [first]."

"I got to where I got to, by winning. Being smart. Not working harder, but smarter. So when you've got fighters that say 'I just done it for the fans', that's not true, totally not true. I do it for a little bit of everything. But once again, like I always say, I am a prize fighter. The prize comes first."

"I just truly believe in: if you're put in a position where you know that you can win.. ..if you got somebody presenting a deal that's against your judgement, don't take the deal. Hold out. And that's what I did. That's why I have the biggest deal in sports history. I held out. And I took my time and I had patience."

"The endorsements are there. [But] there is only one endorsement: TMT, The Money Team... And so I believe in endorsing myself...I don't have anything against Rebook. I don't have anything against Adidas. [But] why can't I endorse myself? ...I do have an endorsement deal. I'm endorsed by myself."

"A 19-year career, taking no punishment to the body and making hundreds of millions of dollars. Now that's something to talk about."

On the importance of teamwork:

"Every morning I get up and see my kids, that's what makes Floyd Mayweather want to go hard"

"When I hang out with my billionaire buddies, when I sit down with them, I don't sit down with them and say 'I wanna get on your yacht, I wanna get on your plane'. No, that ain't what I do. 'Ah I like your house!'. No, you know what I say? [I say] 'show me the way. I want to do the same thing that you're doing.'"

"What we believe in preaching and talking about around here is just helping one and another. Because we're stronger together than apart."

"I am always thinking: 'How can I get better?'. How can I continue to teach people around me how to fish and I don't want to fish for them. We teach you how to become entrepreneurs. And if we can't, we want you to be the best that you can be under the Mayweather banner"

"It's not just about me being happy. If I know my people around me are happy.. I feel great"

"I appreciate HBO. I appreciate the media and the photographers, to the writers, to everybody. All the companies. And I really mean that genuinely from my heart and my soul."

On the contracts of fighters:

"Do you know [that] Bob Arum is the middleman? And once the money goes to Pay-Per-View, Bob Arum is going to take the money and put the money in Bob Arum's pocket. Bob Arum is going to say 'I found the venue and I can get the money upfront'. The fighters don't really know what they get or how much he really put up because they don't go to the promoter and say 'how much did they give me for the site fee, how much was it?'"

"I heard that Manny Pacquiao is getting 20 million [for his fight]. But do you also tell the fans that between 23% and 30% is going to you [Bob Arum] and Golden Boy? Tell me the reason why. I'm still trying to find out why!"

"The difference between when I do [fight], I keep all the money. Like, checks be coming in. People don't understand, checks come in for years. You get a check for like, $2.5 million. Then you get another check for like $100,000, $300,000, $400,000. Those are the checks that come in for Pay-Per-View. But people don't really understand this..."

"... now, this kid [Pacquiao] money comes in.. ...So when the money comes in on the back-end for Pay-Per-View, when he fights every time, they tell him he gets a certain amount of money.

Let's say you're getting 15 million. Bob Arum has advanced him a lot of money. So when he advances the money, you go to him and say give me 1.5, then they give him 1.5. Then he goes back and says 'get me 2.5'. Now we have 4 million. So he keeps going to get an advance.

So once he fights he's already got advanced on his money. He doesn't know that the money he got advanced on is his money really, from the back-end of his fight. But he doesn't know that because the checks are coming from Top Rank. So he thinks that Bob Arum is fronting the money. But really it's your money from the back end of the Pay-Per-View. And they don't like me because this is the stuff I expose."

"ShowTime and CBS gave me the deal [that HBO didn't give me] and said 'you can write your own checks'. So when I went over there... I bought myself out of my contract [with Top Rank] for $750,000 and when I left them, with the McGregor, the Pacquiao, and the Canelo fight, I made 750 million, just with those three fights."

On building long-term wealth:

"This is the reason why money matters: without money you can't buy food to live, to be alive. You have to have money to be alive. But I believe in creating generational wealth."

"People are crazy. They don't say anything about the Waltons when they're still building more Walmarts and more Walgreens. Just because I may fight [again], they're like 'he needs money'. I don't *need* money. Because at the end of the day,

I was smart. I made smart investments. So I make millions every month for the rest of my life."

"If it costs 12 million to promote a fight, I'm looking to take that 12 million and turn it into 112 million. As a businessman, I feel like that's my job."

"A dentist makes money when he's working on teeth. A boxer makes money when he's boxing. But with New York real estate, you make money when you sleep. So it's all about making money when you sleep. Once you make so much money, you can't buy more stuff anyway. It's good to be able to put that money up and teach your children so they can teach their children. It's about creating wealth for generations."

"I only own all my masters [financial rights to my fights]. That's never been done before."

"Go there and look at my fights. I got 50 fights and I own all [rights of] the 50 fights."

"I had to roll the dice on something. Just like my career, I rolled the dice and took my chances every time I went out there. I'm not saying I don't take chances, but I take chances with things I truly believe in. I bet on myself throughout my career. I believe in myself and I was my own boss."

"I invest in what I know. It'd be very rough to go into a whole new department and possibly invest in something that costs you a fortune."

"Boxing comes first... ...Because this puts us in a position to have the businesses we have or [put] this person in the position to make the money. Boxing was the money maker. And we use that money to make smart investments to make more money. So it comes first."

"The first time I invested, my first investment was real estate, commercial real estate. Huge, sky-scrapers actually. How I got to where I got to was I looked at certain athlete's career, and I said 'I don't want to end up like that'. So what I did was this: it started off with five million dollars. [I] put up five million, [and] I was getting fifty thousand a month.. ..so I said okay, if it's paying off like this and I gave them seven figures, I said I'm not even going to give them eight figures. I went and gave them nine figures."

"A lot of athletes, a lot of entertainers, think about just right now. They want a Ferrari right now, they want a Bugatti right now... ...I want to live like this 30 years from now, 40 years from now, hopefully 50 years from now. I want to live like this for a very, very long time."

"You can have $300 million but if you don't have a game plan, you're broke. Eventually you will lose it all. So me, I looked at so many different athletes, not just fighters, but I looked at different athletes. I said I don't want to end up like them. So, it takes brains to surround yourself with smart people. That's what makes me so smart."

EARLY TROUBLES AND STRUGGLES

You Cannot Do It Alone

At 19, Floyd Mayweather got his *"first real piece of money,"* as he put it. This was when he began to fight professionally. At this point, he refrained from splashing out on big purchases. He preferred to patiently save his money because *"to have a 300 thousand dollar car parked outside of a condominium doesn't look right".*

This would soon change though as quickly as it took for him to become a champion. By 21, after winning the title, he was a millionaire. He began driving flashy cars and was able to afford flashy jewels. Evidently, being a world champion paid well. Mayweather never looked back, continuing to live lavishly.

As controversial as his displays of wealth were, it was far from how he started. Floyd Mayweather grew up around gangsters, drug dealers, and struggling families. His father was a drug-dealer too and made money on the wrong side of the law. The world he was surrounded by was a working-class one. So, if he were to realize his potential, he would need to surround himself with the right environment.

If you want to be great on a mass scale, then it cannot be done by yourself. You need to build a machine that can propel you towards your ultimate goals. You must build a team of the right people. Then, you must lead the direction of that team so that you and the rest of the team members simultaneously accomplish each other's goals.

Sometimes though, the ego of men hinders their ability to lead a team effectively; their ego makes them struggle to relinquish control to the rest of the team members. This is counterproductive.

Though boxing is a one-on-one sport, a fighter's performance is heavily influenced by a team effort. No fighter in history unleashed all of his potential without relying on other people. If you don't utilize the knowledge of others, you risk not being able to unlock all of your own abilities.

Team members who can take you to the next level include coaches, advisors, and personal assistants. Even if you are a multitalented individual who could do everything, you simply don't have the time to do all of it.

Even if you did do it all, you would spend all of your energy while you did so. The goal then, is to put people in positions to do the things that you need help with so that you can focus on the job that only you can do.

In the last few years of Mayweather's professional career, his entourage grew to the biggest boxing had ever seen. From chefs, to masseuses, to private jet pilots, Mayweather's team of handlers grew to far more than the traditional entourage. Each member contributed to the ease of Mayweather's life, and everyone benefited in some way.

When everything is taken care of outside of the ring, the fighter can focus on fighting inside the ring. If his handlers were terrible at dealing with matters outside of the ring, that could cause a mental strain that would affect him inside the ring.

This explains why Mayweather always acknowledged that he was not alone. Mayweather knew the importance of having team members who were all on the same page. It was always clear that he was appreciative of the value that his team brought to the table.

Hire Masters

Teams are useful because they utilize the expertise of each member. As an individual, one person may not be as effective. However, in a working machine with other units, the value that each person brings will accentuate the talents of the others. Hiring masters of different fields allows you to gain the results that their knowledge earns, without having to spend the time it took to get their knowledge.

A fighter's success is heavily influenced by his fighting and training, but other areas also influence a fighter's career. In every area that affects the fighter's ability to: fight and train better, make more money, strengthen his brand or help his health, there should be a designated "master" there to help him.

For example, a fighter's eating habits are vital. Consulting a nutritional advisor or hiring a long-term chef may make just a 5% difference to the fighter's performance, but in a world where a 5% difference can transform the outcome of a fight, that 5% is precious. Many fighters neglect such matters until later on in their career and they may even go their entire careers without ever taking such areas seriously.

Another department that a fighter may need a "master" in includes recovery. As discussed earlier, recovery is crucial for avoiding overtraining. So it makes a lot of sense for a fighter to hire masters of health. This could include going to see masseuses, or seeing cryo-therapists.

Early on in Floyd's career, he found himself in an unfortunate situation due to his lack of having a trusted master in the area of financial management. Speaking about the incident on a television show in 2002, Floyd told the story: "*You've got to have the right people around you. Certain people around me were making me sign contracts that I shouldn't have been signing. [They] had me in a position with an accountant that was stealing from me.*"

Floyd then went on to tell the shocked crowd that he got the situation under control by employing a trusted manager. His new manager was James Prince, who was known for being a music executive. Floyd knew that Prince had a keen sense of proper business handling and would handle his affairs well.

On bringing him in, Prince quickly took Mayweather's accounts to lawyers and found that he was being robbed. That particular appointment may have saved Mayweather's millions of dollars and a tremendous amount of stress.

Being saved a future headache like this may have kept him from having future training camps being filled with distraction. There is a vital lesson here - treat all aspects of your career as crucial, for when you add them all up, they will have a substantial influence on your career.

CHAMP TIP: WHAT MASTERS DO YOU NEED?

Assess your strengths and weaknesses. Consult with experts who can improve your weaknesses and enhance your strengths. For example, if you have trouble waking up on time for early morning runs, consult health experts who can help you, or at least read books on the topic.

Floyd Mayweather himself unexpectedly benefited from a master who he "stole" from his opponent's camp. In 2014 when preparing for Marcos Maidana, Floyd Mayweather employed Alex Ariza, who used to work as the strength and conditioning coach for Maidana. Originally, his plan was to simply rob Maidana of the chance to work with Ariza's expertise.

However, Ariza ended up teaching Floyd many tips in the area of health. Mayweather also learned how to properly rehydrate after working out. This was beneficial for Mayweather, as he was approaching his forties and such knowledge helped his body to maintain high standards.

SELF-VALUE

Get What You're Worth

Contractual disappointments and network disputes characterized the first decade of Mayweather's career. Floyd had always felt that his value wasn't appreciated by Bob Arum, his promoter, and HBO, the television network he was dealing with.

In the early 2000s, Floyd struggled to get the financial respect he felt he deserved from the HBO executives, despite being the best young talent in the world. In

2006, Mayweather requested higher paydays from his promoter Bob Arum. However, Arum believed, "*Mayweather's expectations were out of the stratosphere.*"

At that time, there was talk about a potential match between Mayweather and the Mexican slugger Antonio Margarito. Mayweather would stand to make $8 million if he decided to go ahead. However, Mayweather was disappointed with these numbers. Although he was ready to take the fight, he proposed that he wanted guarantees of $10 million paydays for potential future fights with Miguel Cotto and Ricky Hatton. In addition to that, he wanted to be guaranteed $20 million for a fight with De La Hoya.

By this time, Oscar De La Hoya had broken off from Top Rank and created his own promotional company. Bob Arum was reluctant to make the fight with De La Hoya happen because it was an opposing company. So Arum stated he wouldn't raise the guarantees for Mayweather's future fights, which severely limited Mayweather's earning potential. These restrictions created resentment in Floyd.

Mayweather went on to say that his worst career move was signing with Top Rank. So, in 2006, he formed his own company, collaborated with Golden Boy Promotions, and secured the De La Hoya match for 2007. Had Mayweather stayed with Top Rank, he may never have gotten the fight with De La Hoya that turned him into a superstar. In hindsight, the decision was one that added hundreds of millions of dollars and new eyes to his brand.

A boxer must understand that although he fights for the love of the sport, the sport today is run by money. Boxing is a business, and a fighter is a worker within that business. And like any business, the business owner will do what is best for their business interests first and foremost. Knowing this will help you to understand the minds of the people who run the sport.

People in these positions of power include promoters, TV executives, managers, and others who are in control of the money. Their most significant influence is precisely that: money. Regardless of their sentiment towards you, they judge fighters based on their money-making potential.

Mayweather Jr., though, knew that he had superstar potential. He knew that he wasn't "just" a great fighter. He knew he could be the cash cow of the sport, if only he were given the support to make that a reality.

Floyd Mayweather had been with HBO since the start of his championship career. It had been a turbulent relationship, with Mayweather slamming the "slave wage" contracts that he felt he had been offered previously. Fast forward to 2012, Floyd Mayweather and Manny Pacquiao were the two best fighters on the planet, and HBO had both of them.

However, Mayweather was not satisfied with the fight deals he was getting. But HBO told him he was crazy. They didn't believe that anyone would give him the deal he was looking for. But Floyd wouldn't let it go, insisting that he deserved it. HBO stood firm in their resistance.

So, after threatening to leave on multiple occasions, Mayweather decided to do business with the Showtime Sports executives instead, HBO's rival. And after more than a decade of trying to get the deal he truly felt he deserved, he finally got it.

Mayweather received a six-fight, 3-year deal that would make him the wealthiest athlete on the planet. And it would nicely cap off the final 3 years of his career (2013–2015). Not only did that deal give him more money, but it gave him power and control that was unprecedented in sports.

Showtime gave him the power to write his checks, allowing him to keep 100% percent of his share of the live gate revenue. Mayweather had transformed into more than just a worker. He had stepped onto the executive side of the business.

CHAMP TIP: ADD VALUE TO BUSINESS PARTNERS

Mayweather understood the necessity of maintaining healthy relationships with the people he would be doing business with. And this was evident in one of the media sessions that took place in the build-up to the Oscar De La Hoya fight.

In the middle of a questioning session from journalists, Floyd Mayweather spotted the executive of the MGM Grand (the venue that was hosting the fight) walking by. A light-hearted Mayweather immediately pulled the executive in close and introduced him to the reporters, going on to mention to the reporters that the MGM is the best hotel in the world.

Mayweather was showing the executive that he was a vocal supporter of their business. And praising them publicly would surely add to their revenue. In addition to that, lavishing them with praise and humor made Floyd more likable, which increased the likelihood that the executive would want to do business with Mayweather again in the future.

If you wish to be a valued partner of companies, brands and sponsors you work with, genuinely support them and actively work to build a meaningful relationship. This puts you in a position where the prospect of losing you as a partner is too costly.

Piece of the Pie

Much of Mayweather's financial success could be attributed to his perseverance. Mayweather saw his worth and didn't let executives or bosses persuade him otherwise. When they thought he was crazy for wanting the most significant contract in sports, he stayed true to his ambition.

Mayweather believed he was as valuable as the executives he worked with and didn't feel as if he held lower value than them. Instead, he saw himself as either a partner, potential partner, or at least a collaborator of the TV company.

Floyd was never in awe of big companies, as he perceived himself to be on the same level. Due to Mayweather's understanding of his value, he was also able to negotiate higher percentages in his contracts confidently.

There are different sources of revenue that a fight generates money from. He negotiated higher claims on all those different revenue streams that his fights generated. For example, sales of live tickets may be one revenue stream, but additional revenue streams could include merchandising or purchases from PPV sales.

Mayweather felt that all fighters deserve a higher percentage because the fighters are the ones that risk their lives in the ring. Mayweather's contempt for the promotional overlords was laid out when he replied to a reporter who asked about his take on the financial control given to fighters:

"I'm the reason why guys like Bob Arum and Don King get mad, because I say that a fighter who goes out there and risks his whole life, needs to get

the bigger end of the bargain. If I'm a promoter, that's what I wanna bring with Mayweather Promotions.

I want the fighter to be able to get the most money. But he gotta be able to work his way up to that point. That's not right, for managers to be getting 33%, then the cut-man 10%. The cut-man wants his percentage, then the team. He gotta pay for camp fees. Then the fighter's left with nothing. But people never realize that."

In the last half of Mayweather's career, he held all of his fights in his adopted town of Las Vegas. Collectively, his fights generated billions of dollars for the city when you factor in the flights, food, and accommodation generated for local businesses. And specifically for the boxing business, in all his matches, Mayweather generated a total of $1.67 billion in revenue and over 24 million PPV views. This record by far surpassed every boxer and athlete in sports history.

So in return, he felt it was only right that he received higher percentages of the live gate revenue (compared to what was normal). In addition to receiving higher percentages of ticket and merchandise sales, Mayweather negotiated ownership of the rights to all of his fights; this included money that came from the royalties for future distribution of the footage.

This allowed Mayweather to receive different checks each month, even after the fight was finished, ensuring that Mayweather would never end up broke. To get out of any financial trouble, he could always just lower the expenses of his lifestyle, and he would still always have new money coming in.

Most fighters rely on saving up their career earnings, when they could also get paid from their work for years after their career is over. So once they run out, then all of their money's gone. And because they are no longer getting checks from their fights (and there is no retirement plan in boxing!), they have no more money coming in.

In the twenty-first century, content can be monetized long after the fight is complete, especially with the digital services now available. A fighter can receive royalties/long-term payments for years if his matches are prominent enough.

However, it is the promoters and TV networks that receive the payments that come off of the "back-end." It isn't in their interest to have the fighters own the rights to the content, as this means that the royalties must be shared.

For example, YouTube is the second most used search engine in the world (in 2020), and for as long as a video on the platform is receiving new views, that video will continue to earn money. The fighter may be paid for his work on that specific night just once. However, the TV network can receive monthly payments from the content from the fight for years.

Many fighters find that in a few short years after retiring, they have spent their career earnings. But had those same fighters been targeting long-term passive payments as opposed to trying to save one-off payments from the past, the outcome would have been very different.

Mayweather knew the type of money that he wanted to make and this is what caused friction with him and Top Rank/HBO. He yearned to make multi-million dollar pay days and he did not stop until he achieved it.

Without a plan, you will end up at a destination that you did not choose. Consider what type of money would fulfill you and allow you to experience the kind of life that would make you happy.

Do not look at what others have made to make this assessment. What kind of financial life would make you feel comfortable and at ease? Set this target as the minimum of what you must acquire and work toward it.

LIFE AFTER BOXING

Financial Freedom

Mayweather gave himself the best opportunity not to have to downgrade his lifestyle after retirement. Due to the advice of his advisor Al Haymon, Mayweather valued being able to receive monthly checks from 'smart investments'. If you have not guaranteed your long-term financial stability, then you have wasted a great opportunity that an athletic career provides. This applies regardless of the amount you have earned in your career.

Mayweather saw the need to use the "savings" that came from his career to invest. Mayweather put that money into making him more money, rather than spending all of it and never seeing it again. In other words, he sought out money-making opportunities that would ensure his long-term financial security.

When asked about his monetary expenditures and even additions to "The Money Team" entourage, Mayweather liked to emphasize the importance of investing in assets and not liabilities. An asset is something (or someone) that adds value, while a liability is the opposite (something or someone that incurs a loss or adds potential risks).

Many fighters are forced to continue fighting after they have stepped away because of financial issues, but this can be offset by putting your money to work for you. Spending money on a flashy car may add excitement to your life, but it is an object that loses monetary value over time. So when you decide to sell it, it will be at a much lower price than what you paid for it.

On the flip side, if you use that same money on giving a loan to a car sales business instead, perhaps agreeing to get a guaranteed increased return after some time, then that money would result in an increase to your bank account. The difference is that in the first example, money was spent, but in the second example, money was invested. After rising in value like this, it could then be traded back into the form of cash/money, at a higher price than at the start.

Long-term investing is not a concept that fighters consider. It is no surprise that so many athletes have a history of becoming penniless soon after their retirement. They are taught to focus on fighting for one slice of the pie, not knowing they can have the other slices too.

There isn't just one way to receive income though; there are multiple forms of income. The following section will detail the different ways that money can be brought in. Understanding this will give you the best chance of making a financial success out of your career efforts. Your work deserves it.

CHAMP TIP: MONEY MANAGEMENT

1. After receiving paydays, ensure that you set some aside for tax purposes.

2. Work to build up a healthy savings account (e.g. save six months worth of living expenses)

3. Set up a state-recognized company/ LLC, so you are able to claim fees, equipment, and all purchases related to your fighting as a business expense.

4. Hire an accountant, and do occasional audits.

5. Once you start earning large paydays, add a financial advisor and financial lawyer to the team. Manage your money wisely and ensure you are not overspending or being taken advantage of.

Disclaimer: This is not financial instruction. These points are only general guidelines and topics to dig deeper in to. Please do your own research regarding the official tax/company laws of your specific state and country.

Different Types of Income

Employee-Paid – "Talk to my promoter":

The employee wage is earned when you are paid as someone who works for a company that is already set up by someone else. When a fighter receives money as an employee, it is strictly based on when they fight and never more than that. You fight, you get paid, and for as long as the fighter is active, this can work. The fighter has the potential to earn a lot in this way if he receives enough exposure.

The problem comes when the fighter can no longer compete. Then there is no longer potential for him to earn money. As such, he is forced to spend the remaining earnings that he has saved up in his career. However, the truth is that saving up only delays the time when the money is going to be spent. It isn't going to be saved forever, there will come a time when it will be spent.

Under the employee wage, the fighter will go broke if he spends too quickly. This forces the fighter to dramatically downgrade his lifestyle after he retires so that he doesn't run out of money. Then, when he runs out, he will have to go out and earn money again. This is why many retired fighters are forced to come back and fight, despite them knowing they are not as physically effective as before. The employee wage is a continuous race away from an empty bank account.

Self-Made – "I'm in control":

The responsibility that a business or a company takes on is one of the reasons that employees like being the employee. They only have to carry out the routine of work, without the intuitiveness that the company leaders need. However, a person in a self-employed position likes taking on that responsibility, feeling confident in their ability to lead. This type of person also likes having control over their own affairs.

In boxing terms, this would be like a fighter taking over the responsibilities that the promotional company or manager holds. Negotiating contracts, sorting out fees and splits with the venue, handling marketing, meeting with TV networks, or managing the schedules of team members are all managerial duties.

The problem is that doing all of this will expend way too much of the fighter's energy. Any fighter who wishes to not stress himself out in training camp would do well not to take on all of the tasks for themselves. This is why effective team building is necessary.

The difficulty of these tasks also explains why promoters are primarily entitled to greater control of the financial gains. Promoters shoulder the legal and financial burdens that come with setting up the event. Though it is true that the fighter risks his life in the ring, the promoter risks their money. Practically all up-and-coming fighters wouldn't be able to put together matches without the promoter's assistance.

Currently, there is no official organization overseeing the entire sport. This is one of the reasons why corruption has been a part of boxing's history. Other sports, like tennis or soccer, have a universally-accepted infrastructure protecting the careers of their athletes. A boxer though, is out by himself and is tasked with the great responsibility of making the right choices.

Business owner – "I have my own company":

Mayweather became his own boss/business owner when he set up Mayweather Promotions. Unlike the self-employed person who tries to do everything himself, Mayweather put trusted personnel in positions to run it for him. This included hiring the services of his advisor Leonard Ellerbe.

When you set up a system that other team members can occupy and run, this allows a person to spread the effort and utilize different sources of talent. Instead of exhausting yourself with all of the tasks, delegate them. This enables the masters of each area to excel, which helps the business as a whole. It also provides security for the leader who set it up. Then, if necessary, the business owner can step away from the business entirely and it would continue to run.

Becoming his own boss and building a team gave Mayweather control. It allowed him to market himself in the way that he felt best, and he also had the power to make the fights that he wanted. As he said, it was only after he left Top Rank that he began doing record-breaking numbers.

Also, having Mayweather Promotions ensured that he could have a promotional career after his fighting career was done. The career of an athlete will fade once their body deteriorates. However, for Mayweather, being a promoter meant that he could prolong his money-making potential long after this happened.

Investor – "Smart investments":

Floyd Mayweather further ensured his long-term financial security by making "smart investments". Mayweather created passive income streams, meaning that he invested in assets and systems that allowed him to earn money without him needing to actively put in time or effort. In short, an investor uses his money to make him more money by lending it to business owners or acquiring assets that other people pay for.

Following his retirement, Mayweather targeted a goal of accumulating a commercial real estate portfolio worth more than a billion dollars, which even included skyscrapers, mainly in the state of New York. Such investments allowed him to make millions each month, without having to lift a glove and without having to run a business.

While fighting is a fighter's passion, the ability to earn money while not having to take punishment is a luxury that a retired fighter can't help but appreciate. The undeniable benefit of this is that the fighter does not have to downgrade his lifestyle or ever risk "running out" of savings when his money is constantly making him more money.

Disclaimer: The previous four types of income listed are adopted by the cash-flow quadrant model, presented by Robert Kiyosaki.

CHAMP TIP: STUDY INVESTING

After building up savings, consider committing a certain percentage of your money (such as 10-40%) to invest. This will ensure the security of your future. Study the different types of assets that you can accumulate (stocks, bonds, gold, crypto-currency, properties, business-lending) and the different ways in which you can get paid for it (monthly, quarterly, etc.).

CONCLUSION

After defeating Pacquiao and Berto in his 48th and 49th fights in 2015, Floyd Mayweather equaled the legendary heavyweight champ Rocky Marciano's 49-0 record. Such a record is truly a rarity.

Floyd had beaten and conquered enough fighters in his generation to prove that he deserved to be considered as the best fighter of his era, and one of the best athletes overall. Floyd felt he had *'accomplished all I had to accomplish,'* and, in 2015, at the end of his spectacular six-fight Showtime contract, he retired from the sport.

That was until two years later, when the challenge from Conor McGregor arose. McGregor was the most famous fighter in the MMA game and had an outspoken attitude, just like Mayweather. Conor McGregor publicly challenged Mayweather to a boxing match via interviews and social media. This prompted Mayweather to agree to come back for one more fight on August 26th of 2017.

The fight would cap off his record to the rounded number of '50' if Mayweather were to win. The two were both magnificent trash talkers, so the press conferences were the most exciting pieces of theatre that the boxing world had ever seen.

Floyd had never been up against a fighter who was as confident as McGregor was, and as we have learned from chapter 3, this would entice casual fans into watching the fight. Many people genuinely believed that Mayweather had met his match, after seeing the confidence of Conor.

However, the vast majority of the boxing insiders felt that this match was a disrespect to the boxing world. They believed that Mayweather would dismissively finish Conor. They felt that someone who had never even had a boxing match before should never have been granted the opportunity to step inside the ring with Floyd.

There were even calls from some boxing critics to demote the fight to an unofficial exhibition. Many others felt that Mayweather did not deserve to cash in on what would be one of the biggest sporting events in history. And though one could understand why they would feel that way, it is important to remember the work Mayweather had gone through to get to that point.

The fight between Mayweather and McGregor became the second event to cross the 4+ million mark in PPV sales. The bout accumulated 4.3 million worldwide PPV purchases. Though the live gate revenue ($55 million generated) was not as high as the Pacquiao fight ($72 million), Mayweather still walked away with around $275 million after all was said and done!

In the fight, Mayweather put on an exciting show, eventually finishing McGregor in ten rounds when the referee stopped the fight. As distasteful as it could be seen to be, and as easy as it now seemed for Mayweather to pick up such checks, the struggles of his career must not be forgotten.

As crazy as it may have seemed for Mayweather to command such a payday from an inexperienced opponent, he had earned that right. There were calls for

Mayweather to rematch Canelo instead. Canelo had risen to the top of many of the critic's rankings in 2017.

However, Mayweather knew that fighting Canelo again wouldn't give him the full credit that would've been deserved anyway - there would just never be a point where his critics would submit and say 'he's done enough'.

However, with McGregor, although he would receive less approval, he would receive more millions. At the end of a fighter's career, that is what boxing is; a business. Mayweather's career is an inspirational case to look at because, as glamorous as it seemed in the end, it required the intricacy of a scientist in the beginning.

Mayweather is an example to many fighters who need to mimic aspects of his success to manifest their own greatness. At times, you may feel that many outsiders will not see the truth of your value, but you must demand that it be seen. One shouldn't demand it by just saying it, but be willing to endure the process to acquire the necessary skills that will enable you to defeat the relevant obstacles so it can happen. This goes for anything in life.

Had Mayweather conceded to *Top Rank* when they made him second priority to Oscar De La Hoya, who was the star at that time, then we would not have seen a fighter make a billion dollars in his career. Even more remarkably, Mayweather did it without the backing of huge companies sponsoring him. Instead, he sponsored himself and invested his own money into his career.

CONCLUSION

Although it doesn't feel like it, being a boxer is simply a job. The difference is that the earning potential and the feeling of fulfillment a fighter can get is limitless. However, the job is one that is usually limited to just two decades.

Unlike people in a regular job, a fighter gets to live out his dream and do what he loves. That in itself is a luxury that many people will never experience. So, you must treat it with the level of commitment it deserves. Observe the discipline which Mayweather had for the game and follow his example.

Many readers will learn about the intensity that Mayweather attacked his craft with and say, *'wow, that's great. But my situation is different'*. These are excuses and false justifications. The goal is to adopt some of his habits so that you can take control of your destiny too. It isn't enough to watch in admiration from the side-lines. You must take the risk, step on the canvas, and be one that others can also admire.

"Like Ali, a lot of people didn't like Ali in the beginning, but in the end.. ..Once my career is over and I'm long gone, don't show me love and respect me 50 years from now. Show me it now while I'm in this sport. Embrace me, show me love, I'm a good fighter" - Floyd Mayweather

RECORD & ACHIEVEMENTS

RECORD

1996 (Debut)

FIGHT NO.	OPPONENT	RESULT	DATE	OTHER
1	Roberto Apodaca (0-0)	TKO 2/4	Oct. 11	Debut at super featherweight (130lb)
2	Reggie Sanders (1-1)	UD 4/4	Nov. 30	

1997 (Learning in the pro ranks)

FIGHT NO.	OPPONENT	RESULT	DATE
3	Jerry Cooper (6-3)	TKO 1/6	Jan. 18
4	Edgar Ayala (0-0)	TKO 2/4	Feb. 1
5	Kino Rodriguez (9-9-2)	TKO 1/6	Mar. 3
6	Bobby Giepert (19-8)	TKO 1/6	Apr. 12
7	Tony Duran (12-15-1)	TKO 1/6	May 9
8	Larry O'Shieds (12-3-1)	UD 6/6	Jun. 14
9	Jesus Chavez (1-13-1)	TKO 5/6	Jul. 12
10	Louie Leija (18-3-1)	TKO 2/10	Sep. 6
11	Felipe Garcia (14-19-1)	KO 6/8	Oct. 14
12	Angel Nunez (14-11-3)	TKO 3/8	Nov. 20

1998 (Title push)

FIGHT NO.	OPPONENT	RESULT	DATE	OTHER
13	Hector Arroyo (16-4-2)	TKO 5/10	Jan. 9	
14	Sam Girard (17-4-1)	KO 2/10	Feb. 28	
15	Miguel Melo (8-1)	TKO 3/10	Mar. 23	
16	Gustavo Cuello (20-7)	UD 10/10	Apr. 18	
17	Tony Pep (38-6)	UD 10/10	Jun. 14	
18	Genaro Hernandez (38-1-1)	RTD 8/12	Oct. 3	Won the WBC World Super featherweight title (130 lb.)
19	Angel Manfredy (25-2-1)	TKO 2/12	Dec. 19	1st title defense

1999 (Title defenses)

FIGHT NO.	OPPONENT	RESULT	DATE	OTHER
20	Carlos Rios (44-2-1)	UD 12/12	Feb. 17	2nd title defense
21	Justin Juuko (33-2-1)	KO 9/12	May 22	3rd title defense
22	Carlos Genera (34-2-0)	RTD 7/12	Sep 11	4th title defense

2000-2004 (Dominating all challengers and moving up in weight)

FIGHT NO.	OPPONENT	RESULT	DATE	OTHER
23	Gregorio Vargas (40-6-1)	UD 12/12	Mar. 18	5th title defense

24	Emmanuel Augustus (22-16-4)	TKO 9/10	Oct. 21 '00	Tune-up after lay-off
25	Diego Corrales (33-0)	TKO 10/12	Jan. 20 '01	6th title defense
26	Carlos Hernandez (33-2-1)	UD 12/12	May 26 '01	7th title defense
27	Jesus Chavez (35-1)	RTD 9/12	Nov. 10 '01	8th title defense
28	Jose Luis Castillo (45-4-1)	UD 12/12	Apr. 20 '02	Wins WBC Lightweight title (135 lb.)
29	Jose Luis Castillo (46-5-1)	UD 12/12	Dec. 7 '02	1st title defense
30	Victoriano Sosa (35-2-2)	UD 12/12	Apr. 19 '03	2nd title defense
31	Philip Ndou (31-1)	TKO 7/12	Nov. 1 '03	3rd title defense
32	DeMarcus Corley (28-2-1)	UD 12/12	May 22 '04	WBC Light Welterweight eliminator

2005-2007 (Reaching stardom)

FIGHT NO.	OPPONENT	RESULT	DATE	OTHER
33	Henry Bruseles (21-2-1)	TKO 8/12	Jan. 22 '05	WBC Light Welterweight eliminator
34	Arturo Gatti (39-6)	RTD 6/12	Jun. 25 '05	Won WBC Light Welterweight title (140lb)
35	Sharmba Mitchell (56-4)	TKO 6/12	Nov. 19 '05	Welterweight debut (147lb)
36	Zab Judah (34-3)	UD 12/12	Apr. 9 '06	IBF Welterweight title Vacant IBO Welterweight title
37	Carlos Baldomir (43-9-6)	UD 12/12	Nov. 4 '06	IBO Welterweight title defense WBC Welterweight title IBA Welterweight title
38	Oscar De La Hoya (38-4)	SD 12/12	May 5 '07	WBC Light Middleweight title (154lb)
39	Ricky Hatton (43-0)	TKO 10/12	Dec. 8 '07	WBC Welterweight title defense

2009-2017 (HBO PPV mega-events)

FIGHT NO.	OPPONENT	RESULT	DATE	OTHER
40	Juan Manuel Marquez (50-4-1)	UD 12/12	Sep. 19 '09	Comeback fight at welterweight limit
41	Shane Mosley (46-5)	UD 12/12	May 1 '10	
42	Victor Ortiz (29-2-2)	KO 4/12	Sep. 17 '11	WBC Welterweight title
43	Miguel Cotto (37-2)	UD	May 5 '12	Super WBA Light Middleweight

	12/12		Title

2013-2017 (Showtime PPV years)

FIGHT NO.	OPPONENT	RESULT	DATE	OTHER
44	Robert Guerrero (31-1-1)	UD 12/12	May 4 '13	WBC Welterweight title defense
45	Saul 'Canelo' Alvarez (42-0-1)	MD 12/12	Sep. 14 '13	WBC Light Middleweight title
				Super WBA Light Middleweight Title defense
46	Marcos Maidana (35-3)	MD 12/12	May 3 '14	WBC Welterweight title defense
				Super WBA Welterweight title
47	Marcos Maidana 2 (35-4)	UD 12/12	Sep. 13 '14	WBC Welterweight title defense
				WBC Super Welterweight title defense
				Super WBA Welterweight title defense
48	Manny Pacquiao (57-5-2)	UD 12/12	May 2 '15	Super WBC Welterweight title defense
				WBC Welterweight title defense
				WBO Welterweight title
49	Andre Berto (30-3)	UD 12/12	Sep. 12 '15	Super WBA Welterweight title defense
				WBC Welterweight title defense
50	Conor McGregor (0-0)	TKO 10/12	Aug. 26 '17	

ACHIEVEMENTS & FACTS

Fighting family:
Son of boxer-trainer Floyd Mayweather Sr.
Nephew of boxers Roger Mayweather & Jeff Mayweather
Half-brother of boxer Justin Mayweather Jones

Title fights
- 26-0 (10KO) in title fights
- 23-0 (9KO) in lineal title fights

RECORD & ACHIEVEMENTS

- 24-0 (7KO) against former/ current titlists
- Record of 4-0 (1KO) against Hall of Famers

Major titles
- WBC super featherweight title ('98-'02, 8 defenses)
- WBC lightweight title 2002-2004

Minor titles
- IBO welterweight title (April 06)
- IBA welterweight title (November 06)
- WBC Diamond super-welterweight title (May 2012)

Awards - Notable awards
Boxing Writers Association of America - Fighter of the Year (2007, 2013, 2015)
Boxing Writers Association of America - Fighter of the decade (2010-2019)
The Ring Magazine - Fighter of the Year (1998, 2007)
The Ring Magazine - Event of the Year (2007. 2008, 2010, 2013, 2015)
The Ring Magazine - Comeback of the Year (2009)
Sports Emmy Award for Outstanding Edited Sports Coverage (2014; Executive Producer for Mayweather vs Canelo, Epilogue)
Sports Emmy Award for Outstanding Edited Sports Coverage (2016; Executive Producer for Mayweather vs Berto, Epilogue)

Awards - Notable Achievements
- First American amateur boxer to defeat a Cuban in 20 years, after defeating Lorenzo Aragon in Olympic quarterfinals at 1996 Atlanta Olympics
- Bronze medalist in the featherweight category of the 1996 Olympic Games
- First fighter out of the '96 Olympic games to win a title
- Youngest titleholder in boxing when he won the WBC super-featherweight title in '98
- Fourth boxer to win a world title in at least five weight divisions (Thomas Hearns, Sugar Ray Leonard, Oscar De La Hoya)
- Second fighter to win a lineal title in at least four divisions
- Holds the record for most titles held (5; WBC, WBA, WBO, welterweight titles & WBA, WBC Light Middleweight titles)
- Shares record for most titles won: 11 (with Evander Holyfield)
- Officially ranked No 1. By The Ring Magazine from July '05-June 2008 & December 2012-September 2015

Forbes Magazine annual list of highest-paid athletes:
2007: No. 16 - $26.5 million
2010: No. 2 with $65 million
2012: No.1 with $85 million
2013: No.14 with $34 million

2014: No.1 with $105 million
2015: No. 1 with $300 million
2016: No. 16 with $44 million
2018: No.1 with $285 million
2010- (decade): Over $900 million! (approx.)

Total PPV pays throughout career - 24 million purchases (approx.)

Thank You – *Leave A Review Please!*

Thank you for purchasing this book.

I hope that you have enjoyed reading about the key moments of Mayweather's life and career. By learning about his grind, it personally allowed me to take inspiration and apply some patience and perseverance to my own life. Whether you are a fighter or not, I am confident that there is something you can apply to your own life too.

I would also like to remind you to check out the documentary "The Rise of Floyd Mayweather". It will help you further understand how Floyd forced his way through the doors of stardom. It was created to be consumed alongside this book.

Lastly, if you have taken value from the book, and believe others would too, it would be great if you could leave a review on Amazon. This helps to support and spread the book to those who would benefit from the lessons presented.

Thank you,

Reemus

Stay Connected

Join thousands of fighters and fight fans and follow the brand on social media:

'The Cus D'Amato Mind' Book – *If you'd like to read more content, check out my other book 'The Cus D'Amato Mind'. It is based on the philosophy of Mike Tyson's mentor Cus D'Amato and details how to apply his principles.*

"Automatic Ambition" Book – *You can also check out the mindset-based boxing book 'Automatic Ambition: The Guide to A Champion's Mindset'. It features the story of ten fighting icons, including Mayweather, Manny Pacquiao, Anthony Joshua, Sugar Ray Leonard, as well as others. It is aimed at helping you form a strong mindset, as we uncover the secrets of success from the current and former champions.*

Subscribe on YouTube ('Reemus Boxing') – *A media channel which includes the popular 'Art of Boxing' series, where Reemus breaks down the technical skills of boxers and boxing matches. Also included is the 'Champion's Mentality series' and the 'Art of the Champion' series where we look at the past and current boxing champions to study the traits that led to their success. Other content also includes news coverage, classic film overviews and other entertaining boxing related videos.*

Follow on Instagram ('@ReemusBoxing') – *The channel which covers the latest news. I will also post your videos if they are done well. If you'd simply like to network and introduce yourself, Instagram is the place.*

Listen to the podcast ('ChampSet') – *The Champ-Set podcast is specifically for fighters who want to dive deeper into what champions do to get, and sustain, their success. We go into greater detail on motivational topics and mental strategies to help you be a focused fighter that progresses quicker than everyone else.*

RECORD & ACHIEVEMENTS

Check out the blog (ReemusBoxing.com) – The boxing blog is focused on three categories: gym training, mental training, and history. From articles on how to throw effective combinations and what equipment to buy, to how you can manage your anxiety and what happened when Jack Johnson took on Jim Jeffries, it can be found on the blog. Subscribe to the newsletter to get updates on the brand (promotional discounts, and video alerts).

Collaborations & Contact (Reemus@ReemusBoxing.com) – If you'd like to contact me, I'm reachable via email. If you have any questions or feedback, send me a message. For collaborations and business enquiries, don't hesitate to contact me.

Glossary of Boxing Terms:

Boxing record - A boxer's record is his win to lose ratio. For example, if a fighter has won 38 matches and lost two, his record would read 38-2 (or may be referred to as thirty-eight-and-four). If he has won 38, lost 2, and drew 1, it would read: 38-2-1 (and would be verbally referred to as (thirty-eight-four-and-one)

Casual fans - Referring to a fan who doesn't keep up with the sport, but usually watches fights if they are between the top guys out there.

CompuBox - A computerized counting system run by two operators to record the punches in the match. The system records the jabs that each fighter throws and lands. It also records the number of power punches thrown and landed by each fighter.

Don King - The boxing promoter, famous for his involvement with some of the biggest names in the sport. He is known for his controversial persona and his notorious reputation in the fight game. Despite the controversy that surrounds his name, King was a promoter who revolutionized many aspects of the way fights are promoted.

HBO - Short for Home Box Office, HBO is an American television network. Up until 2018, 'HBO Boxing' hosted thousands of epic boxing matches.

Live gate revenue - The sum money generated from the sale of tickets for the live attendance of an event.

Majority decision (MD) – When two out of the three officiating judges pick one fighter as a winner, overruling the other judge who scores the fight as the draw.

MMA - Short for Mixed Martial Arts. It is a combat sport, comprised of various fighting styles. The use of various fighting methods including stand-up-fighting (known as striking), ground-fighting, and grappling are all permitted.

Pound-for-Pound rankings - It is a list used to rank fighters from all weight divisions together. The list is based on the skills of the fighters and their performances in their own weight divisions. The most respected pound-for-pound ranking list is presented in *The Ring Magazine* (see below).

PPV - Short for Pay-per-view. Boxing uses the PPV service to charge fight fans a one-time subscription payment to view a particular match. This is savored for the most popular matches in the sport.

Promoter - A boxing promoter is responsible for gaining awareness for a fighter and his upcoming match. A promoter is in charge of setting up the boxing match, negotiates the payments for the fighters, and is responsible for the legal compliance of the event. Boxing promoters are not the managers of a fighter, and they are not officially obliged to act in the interests of the fighter. Sometimes the interests of the promoter and the boxer can come into conflict when the promoter takes advantage of a boxer's lack of business judgment.

RTD - When a fight is stopped by the fighter's own cornermen, or even the fighter himself. This usually takes place in between rounds, in the one-minute rest period.

Split decision (SD) – When two out of the three officiating judges pick one fighter as a winner, and overrule the other judge who picks the other fighter as the winner.

Showtime Sports - Showtime is an American television network. The network is the primary leader in airing championship fights today.

Squared Circle - A term that means the boxing ring.

Tex Rickard - A promoter from the early twentieth century. Rickard promoted famous fights in his day and was partially responsible for upgrading the mainstream appeal of the sport.

The Ring Magazine - Founded by Nat Fleischer in 1922, it is an American Magazine centered around boxing and combat sports. They have helped 'discover' unknown boxers, uncover boxing scandals, and have covered the biggest fights in boxing history. They began publishing annual boxing ratings in 1924.

TKO - Short for technical knock-out. A TKO is when the referee (or ringside doctor) decides that a fighter is no longer fit to continue the bout. This differs from a KO, which is when a fighter is knocked down and cannot get up before the count of 10.

UFC - Short for Ultimate Fighting Championship. It is an individual sporting organization in the MMA sport.

Unanimous decision (UD) – When all three of the officiating judges, who determine the result, are all in agreement with who the winner is.

Weight divisions - Fighters who are in different weight divisions cannot compete against each other. Weight divisions exist to eliminate the advantage of a fighter being bigger than their opponent.

WBC - The World Boxing Council is one of the four major organizations that sanction boxing bouts. The WBC championship is widely viewed as the most respected title in boxing. The WBC championship belt can be recognized by the color green.